The Story of Bedford

The
Story of Bedford
AN OUTLINE HISTORY

Joyce Godber

White Crescent Press Ltd
Luton

ISBN 0 900804 24 6

1st Edition 1978

Printed and Published by White Crescent Press Ltd, Luton

The text is set in 12pt 'Monotype' Bembo   M893

Foreword

This book summarises the material about the town of Bedford which appears dispersed in my *History of Bedfordshire* (1969). References are given to the relevant sections of that work, but detailed footnotes are not repeated unless extra information is given in the present text. Some account is also taken of material published since 1969, including H. G. Tibbutt's edition of the church book of Bunyan Meeting, Eric Stockdale's *Bedford Prison*, D. Bushby's *Elementary Education* (*B.H.R.S.*, liv–lvi), and my own *Harpur Trust*. It is hoped that the volume will serve as a convenient summary until a future historian comes forward to write a full and definitive history of the borough of Bedford.

For reading the text and making comments, I am indebted to Austin Baker, Patricia Bell, Alan Cirket, James Collett-White, Denis Gilmore, Bill Kuhlicke (to whom I also owe notes on heraldry), Alan Threadgill, and Nicholas Wilde. The North Bedfordshire Borough Council have allowed me to print a list of Mayors compiled by Denis Gilmore.

I gratefully acknowledge the loan of blocks from the Harpur Trust (plates xii a, b; xv a; xix b; xxiv; xxvi a, b; xxvii a), and from the Bedford County Record Office (plates iii b; vii a; viii a; xiii a, b; xiv a, b; xviii a; xx a, b; xxi a, b; xxvii a; xxix a). Permission to print illustrations has been kindly given by the County Planning Department (plate xxxii), Mr W. S. Knight (plate xvi), North Bedfordshire Borough Council (plates i a; xi b; xv a; xix b; xxvii a), St Peter's P.C.C. (plate ii a), Dr H. M. Taylor (plate ii a), and the Trustees of Bunyan Meeting (plate xi a). Mr Eric Meadows took the photographs for plates vi a, b, and all photographs supplied by the County Record Office were taken by the County Council photographer, Mr K. Whitbread.

I owe a great debt to Alan Cirket for taking charge of the illustrations.

JOYCE GODBER

Contents

Illustrations in the Art Section

Arms and Seals

Per pale argent and gules, a fesse azure.

Argent, an eagle displayed looking to the sinister with wings inverted sable, ducally crowned or, on the eagle a large castle surmounted by two more one above the other of the third.

These two coats of arms were recorded by the Heralds at their visitation in 1566, and the certificate is still in the possession of the Corporation.

The term of anciency means that the first coat was the ancient one, having been replaced by a later one, derived from the design on the seal. However, the ancient arms were revived about 1800, when they were carved on a stone for the gates to the House of Industry, and have been in use ever since. The second (or modern) design was confirmed (not granted) in 1566, and must therefore have been in use then, or a new grant would have been needed. It has been shown in various corrupt forms with a demi-eagle rising from a castle, the earliest version of which appears on Speed's plan (1611), and another has found a place on the Corporation prayer books. None has any authority and none is in use now.

The certificate was produced at the visitation of 1634, and is endorsed by George Owen, Yorke Herald, and Henry Lily, Rouge-Rose.

At that visitation the common seal of the town was noted.

It is assigned to the 15th century by Gale Pedrick in his *Borough Seals of the Gothic Period.* The original is lost, but some impressions survive, the earliest being attached to a document of 1461. The Mayor's seal also is lost, but it too is known from impressions from 1343 onwards. The seals now in use were presented by Alderman G. H. Barford in 1923, copied from the original designs.

F.W.K.

1 Before the Conquest

Fords over rivers offered an obvious advantage in choosing a site for a settlement. When Beda came and settled here, with relatives and following enough for the place to become known after him as Bedford, he chose the north bank. The river would be a defence in unsettled times, but still there might be times when he would journey southward; hence he settled by a ford. When this was we do not know. Anglo-Saxons came, even in Roman times, indeed a few Roman finds have been made in the area we now call Bedford,[1] such as pottery at Putnoe, and coins near the bridge. Finds at Caembes or Kempston indicate a fair-sized British settlement which early had Anglo-Saxon immigrants. In the late 5th century, more and more bands of invaders arrived, seizing land, and fighting the local Britons. Probably at this period the first sizeable settlement took place at Bedford.

In the early years no more importance attached to Bedford than to, for instance, Barford a few miles down the river, or to fords over the Ivel at Langford and Shefford. The river was an advantage for water supply, and for meadows beside it, but not at first for mills, for the newcomers ground corn by hand. Such buildings as there were seem to have been close to the river: indications of possibly two timber halls have been found in what is now Castle Lane; and it is likely that on the borders away from the river the area was surrounded with an earthwork and stockade. Beyond it, such land was cultivated as the needs of the small community required. Whether there were at first local chieftains, whether perhaps for a time there was even a king of the Middle Angles as of the East Angles, we do not know; but within a century the central kingdom of Mercia had been established.

The newcomers were pagan, worshipping Thor and Odin in sacred groves – the site of one such is remembered in the name Harrowden, but there may have been another north of the river.

Some coming and going there must have been among the inhabitants of the various Saxon kingdoms, and perhaps at least some folk in Bedford had heard of the new religion of Christianity which had come to Kent. However, it was from the north that Christianity came to Bedford, for the Mercian king in 653 married a Northumbrian princess, who brought four Christian priests to her Mercian home. From this time missionary work was gradually extended throughout Mercia. As more priests were ordained, a church – a simple wooden building – would be set up in a new area, and from such a centre monks or priests preached and taught in the district round, sometimes baptising large numbers in a river or stream. It may well have been that such a centre was established at Bedford, where the ford would be an advantage, and that baptisms took place by the Ouse. The only Bedford church which we find later served by a group of priests or canons is St Paul's, and this makes it seem probable that St Paul's was the original minster for the area.[2]

THE DANES

For nearly 200 years there was quiet development in the kingdom of Mercia, especially under King Offa (d. 796), but in the 9th century trouble began. The heathen Danes, driven by over-population at home, began to raid the English coast, penetrating farther up the river and pillaging, then even settling. Much of Mercia was overrun. In Wessex King Alfred could not drive away the invaders, but he made peace with them in 886, agreeing on a boundary, north-east of which Danish leaders or jarls would be left in peaceable occupation. This boundary went through Bedford and along the river Ouse. A few years later, the Danish jarl Thurcetel decided to make Bedford his headquarters, and here the local Danish settlers concentrated in war or met for deliberation in peace. For the first time Bedford emerged as an administrative centre.

But Bedford did not remain long under Danish direction. As the Danes settled down and became Christian, Alfred's son and successor, Edward, gradually moved to reoccupy the lost land. When in 914 he reoccupied Buckingham, Jarl Thurcetel 'came and accepted him as his lord, and so did all the earls and principal men who belonged to Bedford'. So King Edward came to Bedford, and stayed a month. Just as he had strengthened Buckingham's defences, so he thought it advisable to develop Bedford on the south bank, surrounding the new settlement with a defensive moat, which came to be known as the King's ditch. Such fortifications as existed to the north were no doubt strengthened, and perhaps a rudimentary street plan laid out. Bedford, like the other burghs established by King Edward, now stood in a special relationship to the king. Usually in such towns the king's representative was the port-reeve. In Bedford later it is always the two bailiffs (originally north and south?) of whom we hear as financial officers. Incoming settlers hired plots for which they paid a hagable rent (haga=hedge or fence). Probably very soon a place of worship was felt to be needed south of the river, even though at first such a church was (as to the north) only of wood. It is possible that before long it was found desirable to connect the two parts of the town by a timber bridge: bridge-building, like defence, was one of the duties for which a man was liable.

The new fortifications were soon put to the test, for in 917 the Danes of Huntingdon and East Anglia, to forestall attack, came against Bedford, but 'the men who were inside went out against them and fought against them, and put them to flight, and killed a good part of them.'

COUNTY TOWN

It is not till 1011 that the word Bedfordshire occurs, but the reorganisation which this conveys probably took place in the 10th century. Some frame work had to be set up in the recovered area of midland England, since whatever organisation existed in Mercian times had been lost in the Danish wars. Thus shires were created. In each shire the strongest centre was recognised as the shire town (Huntingdon, Northampton, etc.) and here it was Bedford – hence Bedfordshire. But whereas as a Danish centre Bedford had looked mainly to the north, the new shire included a good deal of land to the south which had suffered little or no Danish penetration. Over each shire was a shire-reeve or sheriff to represent the king, collect his dues (except in the royal town of Bedford), and periodically hold a court for trying offences or disputes; while if danger threatened, he called out men for the fighting force or fyrd.

Bedford began to develop as a trading centre. When the market began we do not know; markets were obtained by royal grant, but for this early period the records do not survive; however, the well-fortified shire town was obviously a good place for a market. One clue to economic development is the survival of coins. Dies for coinage were produced from a royal centre, but the minting was carried out locally by a moneyer appointed by the king, the moneyer adding his own name and the place of minting.[3] A number of Bedford coins survive, some of the moneyers even bearing Danish names such as Grim and Ulcetel.

With town development came extra churches.[4] There can be little doubt that St Paul's, in its central position, always (when parishes came to be defined) much the largest parish, and served in Saxon times by secular canons, must have had the first Christian church, even though no Saxon masonry survives in the present building. (The lack is partly to be explained by its vulnerability when there was fighting in troubled times.) Equally St Mary's served the needs of the newer town south of the river, and though the first building was probably of timber, stone replaced it as the Saxons learnt to build in stone, as surviving Saxon work shows, found in restoration in 1959. As the northern town expanded, more churches were felt to be needed here, and thus came St Peter's, where the tower is substantially Saxon work, and which may have been incorporated in the town's fortifications to the north. Possibly also St Cuthbert's to the east was pre-Conquest; a water-colour of the old church as surviving in the early 19th century does not show Saxon work, but the Saxon dedication seems to indicate a pre-Conquest origin. This proliferation of churches would be partly due to local pride and the initiative of townsmen in different parts of the town. It is paralleled in most ancient towns, and most of all in cities like York or Norwich.

There was also during the 10th century a small monastery in Bedford.

EVE OF THE CONQUEST

Once more there were troubled times, with a new wave of Danish invasions. Bedford was sacked, for 'ever they (the Danes) burnt as they went, then they turned back to the ships with their booty'. From 1016 there were even Danish kings, until the Saxon line was restored in 1042. Then there were over twenty years of peace until the coming of William the Conqueror.

To sum up: by the time of the Conquest, Bedford had emerged as the shire town, it had fortifications both north and south of the river, and it was a trading centre. Its monastery had apparently disappeared in the fighting of 1009–10, but it had already more than one church. It may have had a timber bridge. And since by this time mills are known to have existed in most riverside villages, it probably had more than one water-mill.

1 NOTES

Hist. Beds., 3, 5, 10–11, 13.

1. J. Hassall and D. Baker, *Bedford: aspects of town origin and development*. Mr Kuhlicke points out that a considerable amount of pottery from kilns of the Romano-British period were found a few years ago, when preparations were being made for building the Bunyan school and centre in Mile Road.
2. Mr F. W. Kuhlicke contributes the following. In the will of the Saxon lady Ethelgifu (980–90), she gives 50 sheep to Bedford. It has been assumed on good grounds that this means to the church in Bedford, and therefore to St Paul's. (Cf. The Will of Ethelgifu translated and examined by D. Whitelock, with a note by N. Ker, ed. by Lord Rennell, Oxford, 1968. The same source gives a list of burial places of English saints drawn up in the 10th century, which says St Ethelberht is buried at Bedford.
3. *Hist. Beds.*, 13, n. 44.
4. H. M. and J. Taylor, *Anglo-Saxon architecture*, i, 58–9.

2 *Castle and Barony, 1066–1265*

With the Norman Conquest came a new phase: for over 150 years Bedford would be dominated by a castle. At the battle of Hastings, Bedfordshire's sheriff was killed, and perhaps with him a few men from Bedford as part of the shire's fighting force or fyrd. The Normans advanced up the Icknield Way, then north through the county, seizing the royal manors and levying supplies as they came, and occupied Bedford; then they turned eastward. William consolidated his hold on the country by two main methods: by confiscating land and distributing it among his followers; and by building castles. As Bedford was in any case a royal town, the former did not affect it, but the latter did.

THE CASTLE

Since the castle was designed to hold down both the town and the surrounding area, the best site was adjoining the town wall, but also beside the river, where it could command the ford (or timber bridge if there was one). Probably some houses had to be cleared, for in mediaeval towns narrow streets huddled closely together. The ground being level, local men would be compelled to raise the great mound or motte which remains today. On such a newly-raised mound, building would not at first be practicable, but it was possible to put up a wooden stockade, while ditch and drawbridge protected the castle on all sides away from the river.

This castle was held for the king by the new Norman sheriff, Ralf Tallebosc. He had a considerable holding in Bedfordshire, some nearby at Cople, Renhold and Goldington, and some further afield, and he made himself felt in the county, both in asserting his own rights and those of the new king.

We do not hear of local resistance, and indeed when the Yorkshire rising failed, and later when a plot by two of William's own earls came to nothing, resistance must have seemed hopeless. When twenty years had gone by, and the Conqueror ordered his great Domesday survey, it was clear that the new order had come to stay.

NORMAN BEDFORD

Bedford, whether by mishap or intention, gets practically no mention in Domesday Book, though details are given of all Norman barons and of the men who held from them in every village. It is only after more than 200 years that a surviving tax return gives us a close-up picture of the county town. But from later knowledge some deductions may be made.

We can imagine a small town. The north is dominated by the castle on its mound, with a wide yard or bailey surrounded by walls. North, east and west of the town we should expect the town walls – much later we get names such as John by the wall (super muro). Within this area were small streets and lanes (there was no square). An indication of street width is given by the present Castle Lane, which a much later map of Bedford shows little if at all narrower than the main street. There would also be little passages and alleys like that still leading to Ram Yard. The houses would nearly all consist of one main room or hall, with perhaps a lean-to outside for cooking. They would be either of timber, or wattle-and-daub, with thatched roofs (with consequent risk of fire): brick and tile were as yet unknown. Later one or two better-off townsmen might afford stone, as did Thomas Aket by 1150.[1] Glass being almost prohibitive, they would have wooden shutters, taken down in the morning. There may already have been one or two public wells for water supply to supplement the river (into which people were apt to throw rubbish). The market (site marked by a cross) was held in the main street, as it still is at Leighton Buzzard; the site was where now Silver Street joins High Street. There was still a local mint; in fact sometimes in the late 11th century there were two moneyers. These were leading merchants who fetched the royal die from London and had the coins struck locally at a forge.

The agricultural land was beyond the wall. At this date we should expect only two fields. One of them, we know much later, was East Field, and possibly another was called North Field, while to the west there was meadow. Almost every family would be mainly dependent on the land; and those townsmen who followed a trade or practised a craft or dealt in merchandise would fit this in with their work on the land. Livestock would be rounded up each morning and driven out to pasture, and collected again in the evening, when there was probably a good deal of noise and commotion. Mills, when we hear of them, are east of the town, and there may by now have been two.

South of the river was the smaller area surrounded south by the King's Ditch, and with a much smaller population, as the earliest maps show.

The whole would seem to modern eyes small and primitive. Since much later we get references to pigs running in the streets, no doubt they sometimes did so now, and poultry too. If we bear in mind that as late as 1871 at Clifton we find references to pigsty and privy close to the back door of a house where many children were taught, we can imagine conditions in Bedford about 1100. Cases of leprosy occurred, a disease which flourishes in bad conditions. But to a villager from one of the villages nearby, Bedford would appear large, rich and important, and part of the growth of Bedford is due to settlers arriving from the villages, as early surnames show. For a burgess, though he might pay rent for his tenement, was a free man, unlike the villager who worked for his lord. If he owned his tenement, he could bequeath it. By degrees it came to be established that if a villager (or villein) owing service to his lord lived for a year and a day in a borough without being recalled, he became free.

THE BEAUCHAMPS

Now we find at the castle a family which was to remain there for 150 years, and to be thought of as particularly a Bedford and Bedfordshire family, that of Beauchamp. Ralf Tallebosc had no son, only a daughter Matilda, and this daughter married one of the younger men who came over with the Conqueror but were not of sufficient standing then to qualify for grants of land. Hugh de Beauchamp, by his marriage with this heiress, was when Domesday Book was compiled in 1086 the leading baron of Bedfordshire, with manors in over thirty villages, from Keysoe and Riseley in the north to Aspley Guise in the south-west, and

Stotfold in the east, besides other property outside the county. When a new king came to the throne in 1087, Hugh de Beauchamp acted as almoner at the coronation. Later descriptions tell us that the almoner distributed to beggars and lepers alms from a silver dish, which he was afterwards allowed to retain.

Some of his extensive estate was kept in Hugh de Beauchamp's own hands; much of it however was in the hands of tenants or knights, who would be liable for military service when need arose.

The conversion of the first hasty structure into a masonry castle was probably begun by Hugh de Beauchamp, and was certainly completed by the time of his grandson Miles.

From the compiling of Domesday Book to the end of the reign of Henry I (1135) was about fifty years. For this time there is little or no direct evidence on Bedford. It was however a period of peace and settled government, and there was probably steady development in the town. A new generation had grown up to whom the castle was an established fact, and who accepted the Beauchamps as a dominant family, and found that the comings and goings at the castle increased Bedford's importance and Bedford's trade. It is possible that there was even a movement in favour of a merchant guild. Such guilds were beginning to arise in at least some county towns, with royal permission, but this cannot be proved for Bedford, where the only evidence is interested hearsay a century later (see below).

CIVIL WAR

The first siege of the castle was in 1137. By this time Hugh de Beauchamp's grandson Miles was castellan. Henry I left only a daughter, Matilda, and an attempt was made on the crown by her cousin Stephen. Stephen, having gained a position at Luton, wanted to establish a supporter at Bedford, and called on Miles to give up the castle. Since it was a royal castle, and Miles de Beauchamp the king's castellan, Stephen would have the right to do this if he made good his claim to the crown. Miles attempted to make peace by himself offering to recognise Stephen, but Stephen did not trust the offer and approached with an army. Miles provisioned the castle for a siege, forcibly levying supplies from townsmen – who had hitherto thought well of him – and from villagers, besides no doubt assembling what force he could from his tenants. Stephen had with him siege weapons – probably battering rams and mangonels, which threw stones. The castle however was too strong to take by storm; its wall, the chronicler says, was strong and high; while even if this had been pierced, the keep was 'strong and unshakable'. But blockade was another matter. The besiegers remained in position for some weeks over Christmas 1137, and the castle supplies ran out. Miles had to surrender, and Stephen's nominee, Hugh le Poer, took his place.

This, however, was just one round in the civil war. Elsewhere things went worse with Stephen, and in 1141 Miles was able to recover the castle and drive out the intruder.

Once again, some years later (perhaps after Miles' death), the castle was gained by Stephen's followers. In 1153 came relief, when young prince Henry, Matilda's son, and an able commander suddenly descended with strong forces on the 'very strong castle, and after heavily plundering the town, delivered it to the flames'. In this destruction St Paul's church suffered severely, and it is said that records stored there were lost.

The town of Bedford and the townsmen must have suffered much during these years of struggle for the castle, and must have taken time to recover in the more settled period that came with Henry II's accession in 1154, and with the castle now once more in Beauchamp hands.

THE FIRST SURVIVING CHARTER

It is in the latter half of the 12th century, when houses destroyed in the recent fighting had been rebuilt, and trade began to recover, that Bedford men certainly wanted to have more control of their own affairs – that is to say, there arose a local association or guild of merchants, who joined to regulate trading practices and to get privileges from the king. If there was a previous guild, it may have lapsed during the civil war. In a lawsuit of 1226 the burgesses claimed that they in fact had charters from early Norman kings, that these used to be kept for safety in St Paul's church, and that they were destroyed with the early charters of St Paul's itself during the fighting at the time of the last siege of the castle.[2] Charters from William I and William II would be exceptionally early for such a town as Bedford, but it could be that there was one by Henry I. At all events, an application to Henry II was put forward. Mediaeval kings were constantly on the move, and when the plea caught up with the king, he was at Rouen in Normandy. Here in 1166 Bedford's first surviving royal charter was issued, at the cost of forty marks. It confirmed the liberties and free customs which Bedford burgesses had had in the time of Henry I; and if there was doubt as to what these liberties were, reference was to be made to a charter granted to Oxford ten years previously. They were: to have a merchant guild; to have their own lawcourt and not be obliged to plead outside the borough; and to be quit of toll when they traded elsewhere.

Of these, the chief was the right to have a merchant guild. The guild was the machinery by which leading townsmen could act. It regulated the town's trade and controlled the market; a merchant from elsewhere wishing to trade in Bedford would have to do so through a member of the guild. It regulated standards and probably fixed wages. It also had social functions which would take place in the guildhall. Any previous guildhall had almost certainly been destroyed in the civil war, and it seems likely that the one which appears on later maps until the 18th century, a few yards from St Paul's church, was built now. A 17th century print, where it appears in the background, shows it as not unlike the much later Moot Hall at Elstow. It had an upper room used for legal or convivial purposes, while on the ground floor were butchers' shops or shambles.

A lawcourt was a source of profit. At this date fines went to the king, but still the burgesses appreciated having their own court. With regard to freedom from toll in trading elsewhere, it was sometimes difficult to enforce this right – hence a dispute involving Bedford burgesses at Yaxley in 1226,[3] when in response to Bedford's burgesses reluctance to pay toll there, it was urged that they always did so at St Neots. But as this grant became increasingly common in charters to royal towns, the whole system of toll gradually broke down.

ANOTHER CHARTER

One important right was still lacking in Bedford at this time: financial control. The hagable, the tolls of the market, the profits of the court were all collected by the bailiffs and handed to the sheriff, who accounted for them at the Exchequer. In 1189 a new charter was obtained from Richard I, stating more explicitly the foregoing rights, but not mentioning any change in financial accounting. Yet in fact from 1190 the burgesses did pay a lump sum (or fee-farm) of £40 annually for their financial dues.

THE JEWRY

As towns developed as trading centres, it often happened that one or two Jews settled there. This was centuries before the formation of banks. Christians were forbidden to lend money on usury, and Jews were good financiers. Thus we hear of Isaac in 1192, Bonefand in 1202, and Boniface and his son in 1251, at Bedford.

OTHER DEVELOPMENTS

It was probably about this time that the stone bridge was completed. On it, as was usual in those days, was a small chapel, where a chaplain prayed and received alms from passers-by for the upkeep of the bridge. Such a chapel still survives at St Ives. The approximate dating of the Bedford chapel (between 1179 and 1194)[4] comes from a charter of Simon de Beauchamp, nephew and heir of Miles, in which he gave the chapel (which he presumably had built) to St John's Hospital (see next chapter). The handing over of the chapel seems to have been something of an occasion, for there were present William Ruffus, the sheriff, several leading men from roundabout, such as Robert d'Albini of Clophill, and Hugh de Oildebof of Colmworth, besides several Bedford burgesses.

From 1166 county gaols had to be built where they did not already exist, so by now the gaol in Gaol Lane (Silver Street) was in existence; thus we note that in 1191 its repairs cost 14s 1d.[5]

When the little school was first set up we do not know, but it was in being at this time (see next chapter).

Thus about 1200 Bedford was developing in trade and in self-government after a period of peace, while the Beauchamps at the castle were looked upon as an old local family, and one able to help on occasion. The date of the grant of Bedford's fair is not known, but it was probably early.

DAILY LIFE

Some light on daily life is thrown by early judicial records.[6] It was early in the 12th century that the king began to send round period- ically travelling judges (on eyre) to hold the pleas of the crown. From 1194 a coroner was appointed to keep the pleas of the crown; there was one for the county and a separate one for Bed- ford. The eyre rolls of 1202 and 1227 have Bedford cases relating to the assizes of bread and ale. As these were the staple foods, it was necessary that they should be of the right quality and price, and sold by true measure. Some bakers were in trouble in 1227, Simon Brodehe and three others. In 1202 the wardens of measures had found Matilda in the act of selling ale with a false gallon. Clarice was likewise accused; she was said to be selling three gallons for a penny; but she brought twelve oath-helpers who maintained that she was trustworthy. In 1227 there had been an escape from the gaol of 'tramping thieves'. There had been cases of violence – Oliver Motin in 1247 was set upon by four others. And there are instances in the same year of offenders taking sanctuary in churches (St Paul and St Mary) when the hue and cry was raised against them.

Incidentally, it seems from the town's representatives at the eyre that at this date the town's chief representative (probably the chief officer of the merchant guild) still had the Saxon title of alderman. He was also supported at the eyre by the two bailiffs.

THE LAST SIEGE

Now was to come another period of uncertainty, and with it the last siege of Bedford castle.[7] In the Middle Ages the building up of strong central government by an able king was periodically interrupted when an ineffective or erratic monarch was challen- ged by restless barons. So it was now in the reign of King John, who succeeded in 1199. He fought an unsuccessful war to defend Normandy, and as English barons did not fully support him in it he recruited foreign mercenaries, such as Falkes de Breauté from Poitou. When he came home to find the barons restive he brought his mercenaries here. The northern barons decided to march south to force concessions from him, and as they came to Bedford they were welcomed at the castle by young William de Beauchamp (son of Simon). Did the townsmen see this gathering with foreboding, and fear that troubled times were coming? The barons forced from the king a charter of rights, and thus was signed Magna Carta in 1215. But the confrontation between the king and barons continued, and in that same year, during William de Beauchamp's absence from Bedford, troops under Falkes de Breauté occupied Bedford castle. King John made him castellan, and ordered the castle to be strengthened (this was partly done by stone from St Paul's church). Falkes remained in occupation for nine years, and no doubt made the castle one of the most effective of its day.

He had need to be on the defensive, for King John died in 1216, and the new king, Henry III, was but nine years old. Falkes was on the young king's council, and active in putting down the opposing barons. No doubt his position was not easy at Bedford, but his arbitrary actions far and wide were more like those of a professional soldier in an occupied country than like those of a king's representative at home. Luton and St Albans suffered from him, and resisters were brought to Bedford castle. He acted as if he were above the law, and when the news was brought to him in his absence that the judges in 1224 had the firmness to find him guilty on thirty charges of violence, he sent orders to his brother at the castle to seize the judges and bring them to Bedford castle in chains. Thus Henry de Braybrook was brought to Bedford as a prisoner, and his wife hastened to plead her husband's case in tears before the young king.

This outright defiance meant that the king must act even against one who had been his father's loyal supporter and a help in securing his own succession. Falkes himself, realising that he had overstepped the mark, fled to Wales. The king commanded siege supplies from nearby sheriffs, such as mangonels and catapults, and suitable workmen, such as carpenters and cutters in stone, with tools such as hammers, mallets, and picks. Northampton was ordered to send 4,000 quarrell bolts, and cord came from as far afield as Dorset. Provisions for the king's own use included wine and spices; and arrangements were even made for greyhounds for sport in the intervals of the siege.

The siege lasted nearly two months. The castle now consisted of the massive ancient keep crowning the mound; of an inner yard or bailey; and of an outer bailey where there were outhouses for corn and hay, horses and other livestock, and arms. The whole was surrounded by an outer wall, with towers both east and west. The attackers built two wooden towers, higher than the walls, from which archers shot at the garrison within. Meanwhile mangonels, or siege machines, continually battered the outer wall.[8] At the same time, other workmen were engaged in undermining the walls. The outer wall was pierced and access gained to the outer yard, where the outhouses were burned. Then a breach was made on the west, and entry gained to the inner bailey, the fighting growing ever more desperate. At last on 14 August, the keep having been undermined, the timber props were fired, smoke issued forth, and cracks appeared in its walls. Surrender was made, the royal flag hoisted, and the prisoners, including Henry de Braybrook, released. Practically the whole of the garrison (80) were hanged, including Falkes' brother William. Falkes himself later surrendered and was exiled. He died soon afterwards abroad, it was said by poisoning.

THE END OF THE BEAUCHAMPS

The sheriff was ordered to fill in the trenches and level the ground It was not practicable to level the mound, which remains to this day. He was also to reduce the walls to half their height, leaving only one tower. Some of the stone was given to local monasteries, and some to William de Beauchamp, who was allowed to build a dwelling house, but it must not be crenellated. He protested and made difficulties, but the days of Bedford castle were over. He died in 1260, soon followed by his son. In 1265 the Beauchamp lands were divided among three sisters, co-heiresses. The great days of the barony of Bedford were over too.

2 NOTES

Hist. Beds., 16, 26, 48, 50–56.
1. *B.H.R.S.*, xiii, 110.
2. *Curia Regis Rolls*, xii, 513.
3. *B.H.R.S.*, iii, 202.
4. *B.H.R.S.*, ix, 180.
5. *B.H.R.S.*, vii, 54.
6. *B.H.R.S.*, i, 245; iii, 173; xxi, 193, 195, 197, 202.
7. See in particular *V.C.H.* iii, 10; *B. Mag.* 14, 183–90.
8. Mr Kuhlicke points out that some 'cannon-balls' used in the siege were found in the moat of the castle keep, when it was recently excavated.

3   Churches and Religious Houses, 1066–1485

By the Norman Conquest, the areas of the parishes were probably approximately established, though not finally, for there were still variations to come. Much the largest parish was St Paul's, its church served by secular canons – that is to say, each canon lived in his own residence and had land (a prebend) for his maintenance. Of these canons there seem to have been six: we know the names of two of them in 1066, Osmund and Ansfrid – Ansfrid had land at Biddenham enough for two oxen to plough, and also meadow. In addition to St Paul's, there were the churches of St Peter and St Mary, and probably St Cuthbert. A later account of this last parish (about 1200) describes it as almost entirely agricultural, especially Upper Hayland and Lower Hayland; one of its boundaries was then 'near the castle' and another 'next the cross'.[1] Two other churches may have arisen before the Conquest, or, if not, within the next century: a second church dedicated to St Peter and standing opposite St Mary's; and north of the river that of All Saints, later united with St Paul's but recalled by the street of All Hallows.

THE DIOCESE

The Norman Conquest brought activity and reorganisation. The diocese to which Bedford (with the rest of the county) belonged in 1066 was that formerly of Leicester, but at this time functioning from Dorchester, for during the Danish wars the bishop had retreated southward. The new Norman bishop decided to move north again, and made his see at Lincoln, where a new cathedral was built. In association with this cathedral, various canonries from different parts of the diocese were established: two from Bedford, and the names Bedford Major and Bedford Minor still appear on two stalls at Lincoln. When much later we can trace in Bedford the endowments (prebend) which went with these, we find that with Bedford Major went about 70 acres, while Bedford Minor had less than half as much. This land was situated roughly near the present Prebend Street.

THE ARCHDEACONRY

For local administration, in view of the size of his diocese, the bishop divided it into seven archdeaconries roughly corresponding to the already existing shires, and each under an archdeacon. One archdeaconry comprised the county of Bedford, and here the archdeacon was Osbert. Bedford was now the ecclesiastical as well as the secular centre of the county. The archdeacon conducted a periodic visitation of parishes; and also (since the Normans set up separate courts for ecclesiastical cases) held a regular court in Bedford. When we know where this court was held, it was in the south chapel of St Paul's church, and probably St Paul's was its venue from the first. Here were tried not only purely ecclesiastical matters, but also the laity's morals, including cases of drunkenness, adultery and witchcraft. It may well be that the first archdeacon was one of the canons of St Paul's; we know that in the late 12th century this was so. The archdeacon also supervised the little school.

PLACES OF WORSHIP

Besides the parish churches, two other places of worship are known. One was the little chapel of St Mary in the 'Herne' or corner of what is now St Paul's Square and it was later known as Herne chapel. By the end of the 12th century there was also a chapel on the stone bridge (see ch. 2).

As time went on, the various churches in Bedford, like those in the villages, were gradually altered and extended in accordance with contemporary trends. We cannot see much of this process in St Paul's church. This is partly because it suffered so much in the various sieges of the castle nearby; and indeed when the castle was finally pulled down in 1224, Henry III allocated some of its stone to the repair of St Paul's. Even in later and more peaceable times, rebuilding and extension took place; thus while some of the building as it stands today is of the 14th and 15th centuries, there was also Victorian restoration and extension, when traces of Norman work were found, while two Norman corbels in

Bedford Museum came to light when the roof of the Trinity chapel was repaired. At St Peter's, however, on the edge of the town, what was originally a small aisleless church was preserved as a chancel, and a nave built on to the west. St Mary's was enlarged in the 14th century.

THE MONASTIC MOVEMENT

Bedford's early monastery had been lost during the Danish invasions. Soon after the Conquest a Benedictine abbey was established very near Bedford at Elstow by the Conqueror's niece, Countess Judith. This abbey was given by Henry I the right to hold a fair, which Bedford traders somewhat resented as undue competition – for a fair was an important trading occasion, and merchants came from far and wide. The king had to order Bedford burgesses to see that no harm came to those attending Elstow fair.

Then during the 12th century a new monastic movement spread throughout the country. Sometimes the life of a holy man or woman inspired others. Sometimes a new foundation was due to the king or to a baron who wished to render special service to God. Thus Dunstable Priory was a royal foundation, and Warden Abbey was founded by the local baron, Walter Espec. The various monastic houses throughout the county caught the imagination of Bedford men, some of whom wanted to associate themselves with this work. This happened first in connection with Dunstable Priory.

To give a monastery the advowson of a church was a way of helping it inexpensively. Since most churches had been built as the result of private initiative, the main instigator or his descendants remained patron and retained the advowson, or right of presenting an incumbent when there was a vacancy. This incumbent received the tithes. To assign the advowson to a monastery meant that the latter would have a right to the tithes, or at least the great tithes of corn and hay, leaving the small tithes to a vicar. Abel son of Roland gave to Dunstable Priory the advowson of St Cuthbert's church. Dunstable Priory was also given the advowson of that church of St Peter south of the river, and it became known as St Peter Dunstable, while St Peter north of the river was called St Peter Merton, for that advowson went to Merton Priory in Surrey. At one time Dunstable Priory even contested against the bishop the advowson of St Mary, but this was settled in the bishop's favour in 1200.

Over the years Bedfordians supported other Bedfordshire monasteries with gifts of rents, houses, shops or land. Thus sometime in the late 12th century Thomas Aket gave Warden Abbey his stone house by the bridge, and about the same time Roland of Bedford gave four acres (for which, however, the Abbey would still be liable for the annual hagable of 4d due to the king).[2] Harrold Priory was given a rent of 5s 6d from an osier bed, and of 18d from a messuage by the Severne (a small stream connecting with the Ouse).[3] Sometimes a distant monastery had difficulty in securing its rents; thus Bushmead Priory, which had a house (subject however to payment to the king of $3\frac{3}{4}$d on Hock Tuesday) which it let to Abel Atewater at 21p annually, but when he died his daughter and her husband did not pay the rent for twelve years, and the priory had to make a court case of it in 1339.[4] Another legal difficulty arose over a house belonging to Harrold Priory near the pillory: about 1417 the pillory was moved nearer to the gaol, consequently the description in the deed of gift was no longer accurate.[5]

NEWNHAM PRIORY

Bedford was never again to have a monastery within its own boundaries. That however with which it was most closely associated was Newnham Priory. This foundation came about because of a murder in Bedford in 1164, in which a canon of St Paul's church was involved. At this time there were six canons, Archdeacon Nicholas and five others: William, Gilbert, Philip, Ralf and Richard.[6] Their prebends amounted to 37 tenements and about 130 acres, mainly in Bedford, but some also in Biddenham and Goldington. Canon Philip, who came of the de Broy family of Bletsoe, killed a man. We cannot now know what the circumstances were, if it was in self-defence or inadvertently, but even if the best possible construction is put upon it, it remains an unedifying incident. The case is national history, in that it sparked off a dispute between Henry II and Archbishop Thomas Becket. It must have caused anxiety to the archdeacon, and also perplexity to the leading local family, the Beauchamps at the castle. Something must be done to maintain the good name of the canons of St Paul. The widowed countess Rose de Beauchamp, and her young son Simon, recently come of age, decided to act.

Both the archdeacon and the Beauchamps were no doubt aware that in a number of other towns which had hitherto had secular canons, steps had recently been taken to house such canons in a local community, where they could live more or less as monks did in a monastery. In fact, just as the various orders of monks had varying rules, such as Benedictine and Cistercian, groups of canons were known as belonging to the Augustinian order. It was now arranged that the Bedford canons should live together in a priory; and partly because it would be difficult to procure a suitable site in the crowded heart of Bedford, and partly to facilitate a peaceful religious life, the new priory was situated just outside Bedford at Newnham (at the south end of what is now Newnham Avenue and by the little bridge still called Newnham bridge). Canon William became the first prior, and at a service in St Paul's church Simon de Beauchamp solemnly confirmed to the new priory all that church's prebends and possessions, while he himself increased their endowment, and others of his followers did likewise. Archdeacon Nicholas however, in view of his duties throughout the archdeaconry, did not himself enter the priory, but he resigned to it the care of the little school which had been one of his concerns.

Now Bedfordians had at hand a monastery with which they felt a close link. Over the years many gave to it smaller or larger properties in Bedford. Such properties occupy fifteen folios of the great book or cartulary of Newnham properties which is still preserved in the British Museum.[7] Some benefactors were leading Bedford burgesses, such as Thomas le Mercant who gave 44 strips in the open fields; some were humbler folk like Griffin Walens, who gave 1½ roods of meadow. The various trades were represented among the donors; there was Matilda, widow of Laurence tanner; Laurence son of Robert baker; and there was Walter draper. One donor specified that the rent of his property should go to the almoner who dispensed the priory's alms. Another paid 2s annually to the fabric of Newnham church, and a like sum to that of St Paul. We also find in the Bedford section of the cartulary that in 1359 there was legal arbitration over Trumpington mead; the priory had the right to it in summer months (ie, hay time), but at other times Bedfordians had common right there. And again, though Simon de Beauchamp had given the priory Castle mill, we also find that in 1394 Newnham Priory leased another mill (called Joel's, later Duck Mill) from Bermondsey priory.[8]

A number of benefactors outside Bedford also contributed to the new priory, so that before long it had estates in many villages near the town, such as Goldington, Biddenham, Renhold, Ravensden and Willington, and even as far afield as Stotfold and Wootton.

With all these resources, we can imagine that, in the course of time, a stately group of buildings, with church, cloister, refectory, infirmary and so on, arose in the then rural quiet of Newnham. Some idea of what Newnham Priory was like may be formed by visiting another Augustinian priory where much has still survived.

CALDWELL PRIORY

About the same time, an Augustinian priory was set up west of Bedford, that of Caldwell, which was in Kempston parish. The founder was probably a Bedford townsman, Simon Barescot (this surname occurs often in town records). It was a smaller priory than Newnham, and though it also received gifts in Bedford and the surrounding villages, its endowment was less than half that of Newnham.

An accident at Caldwell is recorded in the coroner's roll for 1272.[9] William le Cupere of Bedford was doing repairs at Caldwell church, with the help of a plumber, and, trying to catch two pigeons in the belfry, he fell and died the next day. On another occasion we hear that the judge assigned to Caldwell money found in the purse of a murdered man, 3s 1d, quite a sum for those days: 'let them be given on the king's behalf to the canons of Caldwell'.[10]

ST JOHN'S HOSPITAL

The 12th century saw a growing impulse of compassion towards the less fortunate, the old and the sick, for whom no provision was made by society, and who depended on the gifts of the charitable, or the alms which monks dispensed. By the end of this century, there was founded in Bedford a home (or hospital, as such homes were then termed) for the aged poor of Bedford who had become poor through misfortune rather than by their own fault. The founder was Robert de Parys (whom we still recall in De Parys Avenue). The aged poor slept in a common dormitory, and took their meals in a refectory. They were ministered to by a master and brothers, and the church of St John was built for their needs. The hospital's endowment consisted of a tiny island within the then parish of St Mary. When recently the building (it later became the rectory) was restored, the beams forming part of the old refectory roof were found.

ST LEONARD'S HOSPITAL

Lepers also received help. Here obviously it was necessary that a hospital built for them should be outside the town, and so there came into being the Hospital of St Leonard (on the site of what later became St John's railway station). This was not popular with the people of Elstow, who were obliged to make a detour on their way to Bedford. The lepers were cared for by a master and six brothers. A reference to Bedford lepers appears in the judicial records of 1227. In those days the cause of an accident was 'deodand' (given to God). Richard of Pavenham fell from his horse while fording the river and was drowned; the mare was valued at 6d: 'let it be given on the king's behalf to the lepers of Bedford'.[11]

THE FRANCISCANS

As the years went on, and as times became more settled, there came a new religious impulse, aimed not at withdrawing from the world, but at living an active religious life within the world, and bringing the religious message home to men and women every day. Those who lived so were called friars, and the followers of St Francis of Assisi were known as Greyfriars (from the natural wool of their robes) to distinguish them from the Blackfriars (followers of St Dominic). It was the Franciscans who came to Bedford. They had arrived by 1238, for in that year the king gave them a contribution – ten oak stumps for fuel. At first friars wandered at large through the countryside, depending on the

Saxon coins in Bedford Museum, obverse and reverse:
   Edward the Martyr (975–8): GRIM MO BEDANFO'
   Ethelred II, the Unready (979–1016): OSWIG MO BEDAF'
   Cnut (1016–35), SOTA ON BEDEFOR'
   Edward the Confessor (1042–66): SIGOD ON BEDEFOR'.

The King's Ditch.

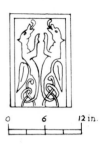

0   6   12 in.

Saxon carved stone, re-used in the tower of St Peter's church showing two dragon-like creatures.

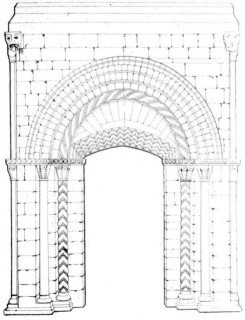

Doorway from St Peter Dunstable, later transferred to St Peter Merton, drawn by T. Fisher, 1820.

St Cuthbert's Church, drawn by Bradford Rudge.

Remains of Franciscan friary, drawn by Bradford Rudge.

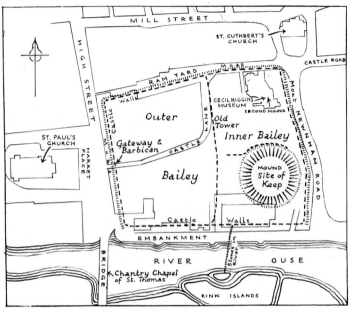

The site of Bedford Castle, showing the probable position of the main landmarks.

Model of Bedford Castle by Margaret Greenshields.

Bedford Castle. Marginal illustrations from contemporary chronicle. (Above) the hanging of the rebels (below) devil offers Falkes poisoned fish.

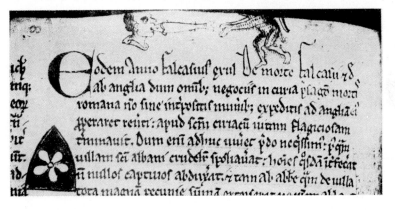

St John's hospital – remains of refectory.

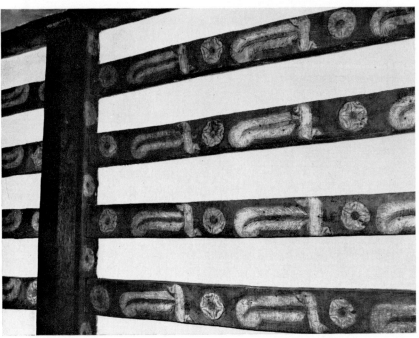

Late mediaeval painted ceilings in St John's hospital.

Herne chapel, drawn by T. Fisher.

The George Inn, drawn by Bradford Rudge.

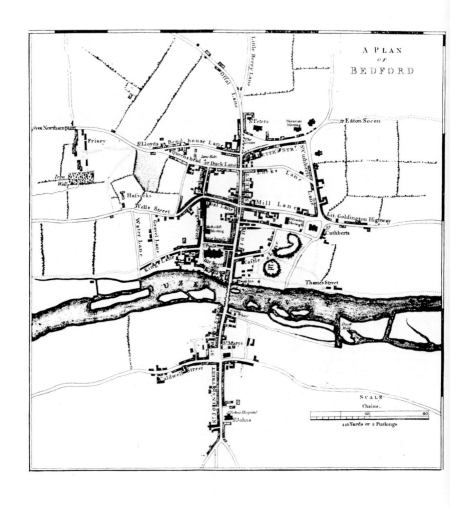

1765 – T. Jefferys.

Two views of High Street.

The old bridge.

Christie almshouses, drawn by T. Fisher.

The Guildhall – in the foreground, Bunyan preaching.

The old Swan Inn.

Harpur's brass in St Paul's church, Bedford, 1574.

Boy from the Harpur children's home, c. 1840, by Bradford Rudge.

John Howard, 1726–90.

John Bunyan, 1628–88, drawn by Robert White.

The Sessions House, built 1753.

Moravian church with dwellinghouses adjoining.

The old Grammar schoolroom (now Town Council chamber).

New (Howard) meetinghouse interior.

Thomas Furnivall, sergeant-major in the Militia, at St Peter's Green.

St John's Street, drawn by W. L. Leitch.

St Mary's Street.

(above) Joseph Barnard, the banker.

(right) Theed Pearse, Clerk of the Peace 1810–16.

Samuel Whitbread, MP, 1790–1815.

Sir William Long, Mayor, 1803, 1813, 1822, 1829.

Bedford house of industry, 1796.

Bedford Gaol, 1801.

Infirmary and fever hospital, 1803.

Bedford asylum, 1812.

St Paul's Square, south and north, drawn by William Dawson, 1833.

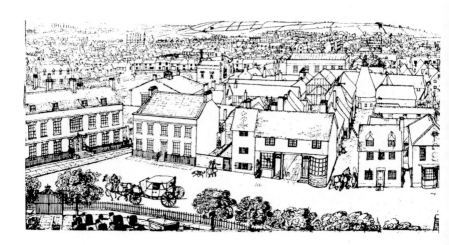

Harpur almshouses, refronted c. 1890.

Britannia Works exterior and interior.

John Brereton, headmaster of Grammar School,
1811–55.

T. Riley, headmaster of boys' elementary sch
1831–69.

Howard the industrialist, mayor 1858–61.

F. A. Blaydes, mayor 1892.

The 'Bedford Times' coach leaving the Swan Inn, 1845.

Cauldwell House, drawn by Bradford Rudge.

Old (Bunyan) meetinghouse 1707, demolished 1849.

Methodist Church, 1804.

Pyghtle Works.

Class at Froebel College.

Sister Fanny Eagles and girls of the Girls' Home (St Etheldreda's).

Children's ward at the hospital.

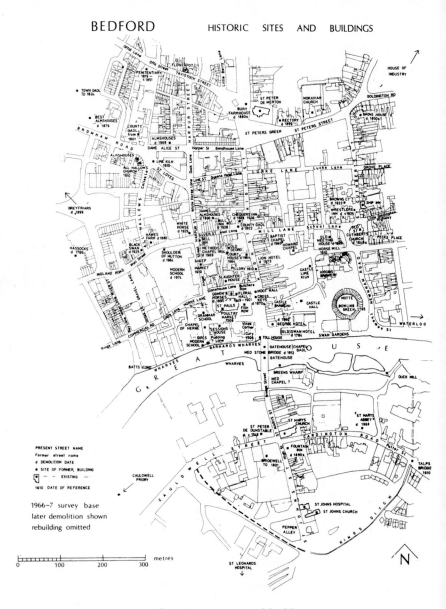

BEDFORD HISTORIC SITES AND BUILDINGS

Bedford: historic sites and buildings.

hospitality they received, but in the long term it proved difficult to depend absolutely on day-to-day gifts, so eventually a house was built on what was then the outskirts of Bedford (near the site of the present Greyfriars). They needed a church of their own – the king gave them timber towards it – and it was consecrated in 1295. When the bishop was in the neighbourhood in 1300, as many as fourteen friars were presented to him – he thought this rather too many. It is believed that in 1324 there was a Provincial Chapter (or general meeting) of Franciscans at Bedford; and it is known that there was one in 1375 when the Minister-General of the Franciscan order came to England and stayed three days in Bedford.

All these religious houses in or near Bedford drew their enlistment both from the town and from a wider area around. From the names of priors we get some indication of this, for where we find from time to time a Bedford man as prior, it is reasonable to assume that a number of the brothers were Bedfordians also. Thus Newnham Priory had a Bedford prior, John, 1283–1300. Caldwell had two, Matthew, 1272–87, and John, 1437–79. At St Leonard's Hospital William was apparently master in 1356. Conversely, no doubt some young Bedfordians with a religious vocation entered religious houses elsewhere.

THE BEDFORDIAN AND RELIGION

What did all this add up to in the experience of the average Bedfordian? Overt religious observance was much more a part of life than it is now, and naturally so, for there would have been none to dispute that 'the earth is the Lord's and the fullness thereof', however ignorant the vast majority were, and however much then, as always, men's practice fell short of their beliefs. The population cannot then have exceeded 2,000, and there were six parish churches – one for about 300 inhabitants. Were Bedford today equipped on the same scale, it would mean nearly 300 churches. Moreover, this does not take into account Herne chapel, and the chapel on the bridge; while there were also the Franciscan church, and the churches of St Leonard's and St John's hospitals; while just over the boundary east and west were those of Newnham and Caldwell priories. And each of these churches would be a far more splendid building than any other the townsmen knew, being large, lofty, glazed, and bright with lights and with the figures of saints and painted walls. Moreover, all parishes had churchwardens; in 1379 for instance we know that those of St Peter Merton were Thomas Roket and John Balle; so a number of townsmen had held this office.

As a man walked over the bridge, he gave alms for its upkeep to the chaplain there. In the town, he might well hear one or more friars giving a racy talk in popular style, perhaps by the cross in High Street which marked the site of the market. At St Paul's church the archdeacon might be holding his court, and he himself might be brought before it for drunkenness or fornication. If he were a well-to-do burgess, and his son was bookishly inclined, he would be glad for his son to attend the little school in School Lane under the aegis of Newnham Priory; or his son might want to enter either of the hospitals or of the two neighbouring priories. If he were in distress, he might go to the almoner at Newnham or Caldwell; or if destitute (and yet of good repute) he might find a place at St John's Hospital; or if he had the misfortune to become a leper, there was refuge at St Leonard's. If he was a felon, and pursued through the narrow streets by the hue and cry, he might be glad to take sanctuary in one of the churches. And when he came to die, he would, if he was a man of any substance, almost certainly leave something to his parish church, and probably also something to the friars to say masses for him: thus William Joye in 1503 left to St Paul's 6s 8d for tithes forgotten, and further sums for the repair of the north porch and for seating, besides 10s to the Franciscans for a trental (30 masses).

Yet one cannot but think that, even by mediaeval standards, Bedford was generously endowed with churches. In fact, south of the river, where population was sparse, it was decided in 1448 to unite the parishes of St Mary and St Peter Dunstable under one incumbent, but none the less both churches still had services in alternate weeks, 'removing every Saturday with books and ornaments from one to the other'. It may be that Simon de Beauchamp's original chapel on the bridge fell into disrepair; at all events in 1331 we hear of a new one dedicated to St Thomas, and in fact disputes over the patronage between townsmen and sheriff led to violent scenes.[12]

There still emerged other ways in which men gave practical effect to their religious promptings. A small man could found a chantry, where masses could be said for a relative or revered friend. There were two such in St Paul's church, one founded by William Joye, and one by the burgesses; and there was also one in St Cuthbert's church.[13]

Yet another late mediaeval practice was to form a religious fraternity, which had special services and also social meetings. Bedford had one dedicated to the Holy Trinity.

3 NOTES

1. *B.H.R.S.*, ix, 224.
2. *B.H.R.S.*, viii, 109–10.
3. *B.H.R.S.*, xvii, 84.
4. *B.H.R.S.*, xxii, 178.
5. *B.H.R.S.*, xvii, 86.
6. *B.H.R.S.*, xliii, 12.
7. *B.H.R.S.*, xliii.
8. For Bedford mills, see *Lock Gate*, i, 66–68.
9. *B.H.R.S.*, xli, 38.
10. *B.H.R.S.*, iii, 153.
11. *B.H.R.S.*, iii, 171–2.
12. *V.C.H.*, iii, 30.
13. *Loc. cit.*

4 A Trading Community, 1297–1485

In the later Middle Ages we can form some idea of Bedford as a trading community. A list of all the men liable to tax in 1297, with their principal goods, has survived.[1] Streets and fields are pin-pointed very thoroughly in 1506/7 in a document which gives the abuttals of the extensive property held by Newnham Priory,[2] and it is not likely that these had altered much in the interval.

TOWN AND TOWNSMEN

Bedford was still largely agricultural. The built-up area (and it was not entirely built up) was within a rough circle, on the perimeter of which were St Peter's, St Cuthbert's and St John's churches, and what is now River Street. Close up to this area came the open fields and meadow: East, Bury, Middle, Oak and Conduit Fields, and Trumpington Mead, north of the river; south of the river the field names have not survived. Practically all the townsmen listed for tax in 1297 owned livestock: horses, cows, sheep, pigs; or had grain stored; thus Thomas Smith had 6 ewes; John Cok, shoemaker, 4 pigs; John Wymund, 3 horses and a cart.

Furthermore it was a small community. It has been estimated that much later, in 1671,[3] the population was little over 2,000, and it can hardly have been as much as this in 1297. The number of men paying tax (those who owned goods worth 9s or over) was 98; there may well have been 300 poorer than this; and the dependants of all these would bring up the population figure to something under 2,000.

What follows relates to the well-to-do townsmen. The poorest must be imagined as living meagrely in one-roomed cottages which were more like huts, and often in real distress.

Forty of the leading townsmen had houses sufficiently comfortable to be assessed for extra taxation, having a good bedroom or chamber as well as the hall or living-room, and sometimes also a larder. Sixty-six had superior household utensils of brass and pewter as well as of wood. Six had mazers (bowls of maplewood inlaid with silver), and two had silver spoons, one of these being the mayor, John Cullebere. The wealthiest was John on the Wall, whose goods came to £6 14s 8d; there were ten whose property was valued at more than £2; thirty-seven at more than £1; and fifty-one under £1.

THE TRADES

The trades they followed were those to be expected in a small town, which was the centre for an agricultural district. There were eleven tanners. There were smiths, carpenters, wheelwrights, and a ropemaker. There were the usual trades dealing with food supplies and they tended to be near each other. Thus the butchers' shops were mainly in Butcher Row, on the north of what is now St Paul's Square; and the fishers (who no doubt fished in the river) in Fish Row; while the poulterers were found in Poultry Market, south of St Paul's. There were also spicers or grocers and a salter. Richard the potter probably lived in Potter Street (now Cardington Road); he also owned two ewes and four pigs, had brass utensils, and his goods were valued at £1 1s 4d.

The clothing trades were represented. Simon Draper's house included a bedroom, and he had brass household utensils; but both he and Thomas Draper were only assessed at 10s. There were a number of shoemakers. There was also a dyer called Richard, who was exceptionally well-to-do; he had ox, cow, horse, cart, ten ewes and four pigs, and his house had a bedroom; he was assessed at £2 19s 0d. Several townsmen are simply described as merchant, and their goods as merchandise.

Though the millers are not so described in the tax return of 1297, three or four mills were still functioning: Duck (or Bermondsey) mill, Castle mill and Newnham mill. The name Port mill also occurs. Later there was a horse mill in School Lane.[4]

A few other documents give additional trades. Thus there was in the 13th century a family of goldsmiths:[5] Alan, Henry son of John, and Hugh son of Henry. The tax return of 1309 mentions a lime-burner called Simon; a later map (1611) shows a lime kiln north-west of the town (off Lime Street); and the 1309 return includes also a scrivener, Thomas, and a parchmenter, also

Thomas. We know that in 1439 there was a candlemaker, William Barton, and in 1479 a glover, John Fisher.[6]

We no longer find Jews.[7] They were always under suspicion, and in 1261 Simon Passelew was ordered to open the chests of Bedford Jews, and find out how much money and jewels they had; one called Peitevin was heavily fined, and later his son Jacob was hanged, while there were riots against them in 1264. In 1266 there were still eleven in Bedford, but in 1290 the king expelled all Jews from the country, and gave to Newnham Priory the Bedford houses which had belonged to Jacob and Benedict, sons of Peitevin.

A trade which came to the fore nationally in the 14th century was that in wool. In Bedford we find Henry Arnold, who was mayor, and was one of six wool merchants in Bedford and adjoining counties who in 1337 negotiated for the king a large purchase of wool.[8] Arnold apparently, like wool merchants elsewhere, bought up surplus wool for export.

Local coins ceased by degrees. After Edward I's new coinage of 1279, mints in smaller towns disappeared, and eventually those in larger towns also.

IN-COMING VILLAGERS

In a number of cases on any list of names we find, the man is described as of such-and-such a village. These place names include all the nearby villages, and some as far away as Keysoe, Stevington, Astwood and Caddington. This not only reflects that an enterprising villager might seek to improve his fortunes in the town, but also the fact that a serf, if he managed to live in a borough for a year and a day without being reclaimed, would thereby gain his freedom: William of Ampthill did this in 1227.[9] A Southill family the Harpers, gradually moved north-westwards, and by 1500 a William Harper is found in Bedford.

STREETS AND INNS

By 1506/7 we get a clearer picture of Bedford streets. What is now Midland Road was then called Well Street, from the well it contained (other wells were in the agricultural land – Hawkwell, Hertewell, and Yrenwell). South of St Paul's, three little alleys led to the river, one called Pudding Lane. Near St Peter's, Cucking-stool lane led northwards to a pond, where scolds or witches might be ducked. There were a number of inns, including the *Bell, Christopher, Cock, Cresset, Crown, Falcon, George, Hart*, and *Swan*. The *George*, on the west of High Street, was a large and important inn, worth as much as £4 annually; while an entry which appears to refer to the *Swan* at the foot of the bridge was only 8s 8d.

PERSONAL DETAILS

Sometimes documents give personal details. In 1414 Joan Ferour, widow, transferred her house to her son; but while she lived she was to have the use of the principal room or another; she was to have food, fire and candles; and a new gown every two years.[10] At the end of the period, from 1500 onwards, wills survive, which throw light not only on what testators prized, but on what possessions they in fact had.[11] Such possessions include (Thomas Joy) a settle, pothanger and spit; feather beds instead of straw pallets; coverlets, pillows, and even (Joan Porte) flaxen and harden sheets; while Nicholas Chapman had no less than six silver spoons, and John Couper had a gold ring. Several owned chests or coffers, and andirons are mentioned. Isabel Wyttesley prized her green gown, while a chaplain, John Syward, lists his russet gown, grey woollen gown, best tunic, and best shoes; he also possessed a printed missal, probably one of the first in Bedford. Another priest, William Golde, had a coral rosary, and a purse of tawny damask.

By the end of the Middle Ages, not only comfort but health and living conditions had evidently improved, for before the Tudor period St Leonard's Hospital had closed down for lack of lepers.

CRIME AND PUNISHMENT

The cases which came before the justices of the peace,[12] who were set up early in the 14th century (at first there was no separate commission for Bedford) tell of some of the disturbances that vexed the town from time to time. Two justices' rolls have survived for the mid 14th century. There were thefts of saddles or of household goods (copper pot and plate). Most frequent cases however are those of violence. Roger Shethere was an unsatisfactory character; in 1356 he drew his knife on William Provisour, while sometime later he and his associates broke into the house of Roger Mayn and attacked him with knife and sword. Another such was Walter le Soutere, who commonly lurked at night to beat people, sometimes with the help of Hugh Werkman and John Maldon, the latter a cobbler.

Sometimes Bedford men caused trouble in the villages, as when Richard Fuller broke a hedge at Biddenham, or William Cartere attacked William Brewstere at Putnoe. And sometimes we find that villagers, after a drinking bout in a Bedford tavern, fell out on the way home, as when Geoffrey of Kempston killed Ralph le Felun of Meppershall with a sickle.[13]

For cases which came before the assize judges, and some of those that came before the justices, the usual punishment was hanging. The gallows probably then, as later, stood at Gallows Corner on the road to Bromham, where this road makes a sharp turn.

Smaller offences such as came before the town court met either with fines, or with simple and obvious punishments in stocks or pillory or by ducking. As we do not find separate mention of the stocks, they were probably (as is sometimes known elsewhere) combined with the pillory, which stood in High Street near the gaol.

AMUSEMENTS

As to the amusements of Bedfordians, practically no evidence for the late Middle Ages has survived, and we must draw on analogies from elsewhere. Since we know that religious plays (rough dramatisations of Bible stories) were acted at Dunstable in the 12th century, it seems probable that from time to time Bedford did the like. Football would be played by kicking a ball down the street. Bull and bear-baiting took place in St Paul's churchyard. References to the butts,[14] both north and south, remind us that archery practice was popular, and indeed encouraged by the government as necessary for national defence.

UPS AND DOWNS

The trading community's development was not unbroken. After the destruction of the castle, there would initially have been relief: no more sieges, nor fighting in the streets, where fires could so easily start. Yet after the Beauchamps came to an end in

1265, Bedford merchants must have missed the residence in Bedford of the county's leading baronial family, with all the comings and goings that implied, and encouragement to trade.

In the 14th century came the Black Death, a plague which over-ran Europe. Bedford suffered badly, for we know that all the clergy died except the vicar of All Hallows, and so did the priors of Newnham and Caldwell. The death-rate among humbler folk in crowded conditions can be imagined.

The building of a bridge at Great Barford in the 15th century alarmed Bedford burgesses, for this enabled travellers to bypass Bedford; and in 1440 and 1462 they represented to the king that their trade had suffered, and their annual payment (fee-farm) should be reduced. In fact they succeeded in obtaining a con-siderable reduction in the fee-farm.

However, in spite of occasional setbacks, and although late medieval Bedford seems modest in comparison with the Bedford of today, yet it was important compared with villages round about, and stood comparison with neighbouring county towns.

REPRESENTATION IN PARLIAMENT

From the time of Edward I parliaments began to be called periodi-cally, with two burgesses from every borough. Bedford was among those summoned. In 1295 its representatives were John Cullebere and Simon Holland. Among later MPs are Simon Tanner, Reginald and John Spycer, Roger Peyntour, William Brasiere, John Glover, and Robert Baker. It is clear that these were actual burgesses: the time had not yet come when burgesses would look outside the town for a representative. Notwith-standing this, parliamentary representation was probably not popular with Bedford, any more than it was popular in other boroughs. Borough MPs knew that they could effect little, and that power lay with king and barons. Attendance at Parliament was a tiresome duty for the burgess and an expense for the town.

BEDFORD'S UNIQUENESS

Bedford's attitude to external affairs might be parochial, but as regards the town's own affairs, some form of self-government was developing further. It was modest, its scope very slight, it was mainly the work of the more prosperous minority, the burgesses; yet the germ was there of something important in our national life. Because, until the 19th century, each borough developed independently, each repays study.

In Bedford it has two aspects: the urge for independence for the town from outside interference, and this comes from the prosperous burgesses; and the emergence among more modest townsfolk of a feeling that they should have rights and should not simply be obliged to defer to the burgesses. This latter group did not include the very poor, whose struggle was concentrated in keeping alive; but rather those who came to be known as freemen, who had normally served an apprenticeship, and subsequently either became journeymen to wealthy burgesses, or were themselves in trade in a very small way.

To get Bedford's development in perspective, we need to compare it with the villages, where nothing comparable could happen. In a village there might be a resident lord of the manor (or, if more than one manor, more than one lord); or if the village belonged to a large estate, there would be periodic visits by his steward to hold the manor court. At this court, there would be some sort of representation; the leading villagers would be a presenting jury to bring forward cases, or make rules about the common; but it was the steward who presided. Moreover, though in most areas the villeins' labour duties had been compounded for money rent, yet much still remained of serfdom as a personal status, and it died very slowly.

But in Bedfordshire there were other trading communities besides Bedford; why were not they comparable? Did the infusion long ago of a Danish element in Bedford contribute to a more active spirit? Then there was the stimulus derived from being a county town, and from the activities that went with this.

Looking at the other towns in more detail, we find some adverse factors there. Though at first Dunstable developed rapidly, and in 1297 had more and wealthier merchants than Bedford, yet it had to contend with a reluctant overlord near at hand. If it were to obtain self-government, it must wrest concessions from the important Dunstable Priory (its position being comparable with that of St Albans as regards St Albans Abbey). Leighton and Luton, though originally royal manors, seem to have missed their chance of applying to the king, and they soon passed out of royal hands (Luton to a lay lord, Leighton to an overseas abbey). If they made attempts to gain charters, we do not know of it. Moreover both had a much larger agricultural hinterland than Bedford, while their trading position was less strong. Biggleswade made a faint attempt to assert itself; in 1294 Biggleswade men claimed that they held by burgage tenure, and so could bequeath their properties by will; but Biggleswade was smaller still, and made no progress.

FURTHER BEDFORD CHARTERS

At Bedford the practice of obtaining a new charter from each successive king continued. It was necessary to renew the charter, since otherwise it might be declared invalid; moreover, renewal offered an opportunity to procure extra rights. A new king was usually ready to grant charters, as they brought in income. The charter of 1227 recognised Bedford's right to pay an annual lump sum (fee-farm) for the royal dues. The two bailiffs were responsible for collecting the dues and for paying over the agreed lump sum. Much later we hear of an 'ancient custom' of the bailiffs holding wassail (chapter 5). Was this a convivial function connected with the collection of the hagable, comparable to the rent-day dinner held on the estate of Victorian lords?

THE MAYOR

In the 13th century we first hear of a mayor. Previously, when the king's judges came round to hold the assizes, Bedford was represented by an alderman (probably president of the merchant guild), the two bailiffs, and twelve burgesses. 'Mayor' was a foreign word, derived from the continent, where some towns were very active at this time. The advent of the mayoralty seems to denote a change in practice. Though we do not know the details of his election, and though the mayor was always a prominent burgess, he does seem to represent the whole town, and not merely the merchant guild. 'Alderman' came subsequently to denote a burgess who had served his term as mayor.

Henceforward any transaction relating to property was witnessed by mayor and bailiffs, so we find their names on any surviving deeds, and have a fairly comprehensive list of both sets of officers.

However, the mayor did not always succeed in asserting the

town's rights. In the 14th century dispute mentioned previously over the chapel on the bridge (the dispute went on for several years while the bridge steadily decayed) it was eventually settled that the king had the right to appoint the chaplain, but it was for the burgesses to contribute to the upkeep of the bridge.[15]

The charter of 1396 is evidence of the power of the burgess minority. No-one not of the merchant guild must sell retail in Bedford, nor even guild members till toll had been paid. It is possible that a newcomer to the town could buy membership of the guild, but normally burgessdom descended by inheritance.

CONSTABLES

Some sort of machinery for keeping order must have been needed as soon as Bedford achieved any size; hence the choice of townsmen to take their turn as constable. By 1400 the town was divided into twelve wards, and there was a constable for each ward.

THE FREEMEN

It is in 1425 that we first find evidence that some poorer townsmen resented their position. The preceding Parliament had had a lengthy session, and the MP's expenses amounted to the then large sum of £11 3s, which was levied on the town as usual. Some non-burgesses refused to pay, led by Thomas Blithe, John Southwode and others. The prior of Newnham was called in to arbitrate. Eventually a decision was given in London by two judges: all must pay, burgesses and non-burgesses alike. The machinery for apportionment was to be as follows: mayor, bailiffs and burgesses were to choose four representatives; the non-burgesses two; and these six were to apportion the payment fairly. If there was a balance, it should be stored in the common chest. The machinery was weighted in favour of the burgess minority, but the rights of more modest townsmen were explicitly acknowledged.

THE CHAMBERLAINS

Probably out of this affair arose the office of the two chamberlains, who kept accounts, and were changed annually. Their accounts for 1507–11 show an annual turnover of £4 6s, and cover the upkeep of the guildhall (where the merchant guild met), its mats, benches, paving, door and hinges. The chamberlains in this period had a new cucking-stool made (5s 3d). New burgesses such as William Duffyn paid fees to them. They paid for minstrels (probably at an annual feast for the guild); they also bought wine for the judge. They kept the town's armour in good repair, and maintained its stock of arrows. And they arranged to pay the expenses of the town's MPs.

But the bailiffs still dealt with older financial matters, collected the hagable, and also took the fines from the borough courts. By the end of the period some court records begin to survive; thus in 1508 six men were fined for having dungheaps in School Lane.[16]

CORONER

Bedford continued to have its own coroner, having done so from the initiation of that office.

THE RIOT OF 1439

As yet, Bedford had not its own commission of the peace, and so came under the county justices. These met, like the merchant guild and the town courts, at the guildhall. Here a serious riot occurred in 1439, occasioned by baronial rivalries. This was on the eve of the Wars of the Roses, when baronial rivalry was joined to disputes over the throne. In Bedfordshire the main opponents were Lord Fanhope of Ampthill (with Lancastrian connections), who came to Bedford with sixty men with swords and bucklers; and the aged Lord Grey of Wrest (the Greys supported the Yorkists). Fanhope's followers crowded the streets and jostled on the guildhall stairs. A dispute broke out, fighting ensued, and eighteen were either killed or crushed in the press. It was a reminder that a town does not exist in a vacuum, and must from time to time be affected by contestants for power drawn from a wider area.

4 NOTES

    Hist. Beds., 52–56, 117–9, 155–7.
1. *B.H.R.S.*, xxxix, 96–101.
2. *B.H.R.S.*, xxv, 15–81.
3. *B.H.R.S.*, xvi.
4. *Lock Gate,* i, 66–8.

5. *B.H.R.S.*, xvii, 86–8.
6. C.R.O., TW 346, 347.
7. *Hist. Beds.*, 66.
8. *Hist. Beds.*, 118.
9. *Hist. Beds.*, 93.
10. C.R.O., TW 343.
11. See *B.H.R.S.*, xxxvii and xlv.
12. *B.H.R.S.*, xlviii, 49, 61, 75–6, 78–9, 87, 90, 93, 95–6.
13. *B.H.R.S.*, xli, 2.
14. *Hist. Beds.*, 157.
15. *V.C.H.*, iii, 30.
16. *Hist. Beds.*, 156.

5 Tudor Bedford, 1485–1603

Tudor Bedford made a long step forward from the mediaeval town towards the one we know today. Its setting was a country more united and under a stronger government than previously. The religious set-up was radically changed. There followed an upheaval in the property market. Some unexpected side-effects came from this, needing new machinery and new efforts to cope with the problems. And in the Elizabethan Black Book we find a developing municipal policy.

In this more stable period, London grew rapidly, and offered opportunity to enterprising lads from country towns. William Harper, churchwarden of St Paul's, and also Warden Abbey's bailiff for their Bedford property, sent his promising son, William, to London, probably apprenticed to a tailor there.

RAPPROCHEMENT WITH GENTRY

The Wars of the Roses had ended the confrontation of baronial armed forces and monarchy; and many old families had come to grief in battle or on the block. True, in Bedfordshire the Greys were still at Wrest, but the 3rd Earl of Kent (d. 1523) was, as his father had feared, 'a waster', the family was impoverished, and his son did not even use the title.

What was more apparent to townsmen was the increased prominence of local gentry. Some of these were already of old standing, like the St Johns of Bletsoe, who were before long to join the aristocracy. Another of the older families was that of Burgoyne of Sutton. Others, like the Botelers of Biddenham, had prospered as London merchants. None was powerful enough to threaten the town's independence. Some had attended the inns of court, and were legally qualified. When legal expertise was becoming more desirable, such men might be of use to Bedford. Some had or rented houses in the town, for instance in 1507 Sir

John St John, Sir Edmund Lucy of Moggerhanger, John Mordaunt of Turvey, and Walter Luke of Cople.[1] A country gentleman might be willing to serve as town clerk, as did William Payne of Podington at the end of the 16th century; or for a small fee to act as recorder, as did Nicholas Luke in 1559. (The recorder was in origin a qualified lawyer who settled cases of particular difficulty.)

Country gentry were also willing to represent the town in Parliament. Local gentry who were MPs for Bedford included George Gascoigne, 1558; Oliver St John, 1563; John Burgoyne, 1563; William Boteler, 1586; Thomas Snagge, 1586; Humphrey Winch, 1593; Oliver Luke, 1597. The gentry were politically alert. Burgesses were relieved of the tiresome responsibility of attendance in London, and also had useful friends when occasion required.

RELIGIOUS CHANGES

That upheaval in the property market, which had given some country gentry the opportunity to improve their position, and had brought new men into their ranks, had also affected the towns. It was the result of Henry VIII's confiscation of much church property. First, how did the religious changes in themselves appear to townsmen, and how did they affect them?

Henry VIII's ecclesiastical changes were carried through over a period of years by a strong monarchy and a parliament which, if not subservient, was not assertive. Moreover, their cumulative and lasting effect was not at first evident: Kings and Popes had quarrelled before now, and had resolved their differences.

Insofar as the new ways tended towards simplicity, one would, in view of Bedford's later nonconformity, expect a climate favourable. We do not know of Lollardy here, as we do at Dunstable, but early Tudor wills give many fewer bequests to Bedford churches for lights burning before figures of saints than is the case, for instance, at Houghton Regis. In St Paul's church only three such lights are mentioned (those before Our Lady of Pity, St Andrew, and the sepulchre); and in other Bedford churches we know of only one light or none. But respect for the church in general seems to have been strong, since most testators left bequests to their parish church, and often to one of the religious houses, while frequently the friars would be asked to pray for the deceased's soul.

As to the state of the religious houses nearby, reports of episcopal visitations in the previous century give some directions for improvement: the bishop did not approve of the canons of Caldwell and Newnham keeping pet dogs, and it was reported to him of one of the Newnham canons that brother John Kempston 'understands not what he reads'. In 1530 the bishop found the nuns at Elstow Abbey wearing scarlet stomachers and low-necked dresses, and reproved their worldliness (Elstow's intake was from well-to-do families).[2] No moral offences came to light. Inspiration may not have been at a high level, but inspiration comes and goes.

Direct evidence of new ideas in or near Bedford comes with the case of George Joye of Renhold, fellow of Peterhouse, Cambridge who was eager for a translation of the Bible, and discussed some of his views with the prior of Newnham, apparently while on a visit home. The prior, who was conservative, was worried, and reported the matter to the bishop. Joye took alarm, and fled to Antwerp, where his translation of the psalter appeared in 1530.

There were those who were critical on moral grounds of Henry VIII's divorce in 1533: a friar of Elstow origin was bold enough to preach against it in London; he got off lightly by being rusticated to the Bedford friary, where his arrival probably produced no little stir.

Yet, as the new policy developed, though in the north of England there was revolt, there was none in Bedfordshire. Thus it would seem that, even if a number of Bedford men were uneasy or unhappy, there was some basis of support for (for instance) an English Bible, 1539, and by Edward VI's time an English Prayer Book, 1549. There may also have been somewhat less respect for the monastic life than in the troubled 12th century.

When we find in 1558 a Bedfordian Calvinist, Thomas Knight, hoping to be numbered among the elect predestined to salvation, and another such, Harry Field, in 1564,[3] it is clear that some ideas of overseas reformers were early known in Bedford (Calvin's *Institutes* appeared in English translation in 1559).

Practical effects began to be felt in and near Bedford. Caldwell Priory was closed in 1536; Elstow Abbey 1539; Newnham Priory 1541. Their inmates were pensioned off and their lands confiscated. The last prior of Newnham, John Burne, whose pension was £60 pa, died a year after his priory closed; he asked to be buried in St Paul's church near the tomb of Simon de Beauchamp, and he left to St Paul's such ecclesiastical 'ornaments' as he possessed. The monks, whose pensions were small, usually tried to obtain benefices, but often had to wait for years, as the market was crowded. Eventually one of the Newnham canons, Thomas Pulley, became vicar of Carlton, and another, John Backster, rector of Cockayne Hatley.[4]

A little group of Elstow nuns settled in Bedford, where the abbess, Elizabeth Boyvill, took a house in Potter Street. Here they had some friendly relations with their neighbours, for one of them gave to the son of the Duck Mill miller a mazer lipped with silver.

The friary was closed in 1538, but friars received no pensions. One of them, Richard Elmer, died in 1543; he was probably cared for by his two Bedford sisters; at his request his best gown was sold for 16s, and with the proceeds twelve dozen loaves distributed to poor folks at his burial.

There were other casualties among Bedford institutions. St John's Hospital escaped the net, and the church with its tiny parish continued to function, while the rector was also master of the hospital where ten aged and indigent Bedfordians lived. But the church of St Peter Dunstable succumbed to reorganisation; the incumbent of both this and St Mary, John Neygott, resigned in 1546, finding the local position too difficult; and the bishop directed that only one of the two churches should continue to function. So the church of St Peter Dunstable came down, its Norman doorway being transferred to St Peter Merton. The chapel on the bridge probably remained empty till a use was found for it as the town lock-up (1589). Herne chapel stood neglected, except for such purposes as the Assizes. No more is heard of All Hallows.

Under Edward VI Bedford felt the effect of still further change. Church plate was now taken – chalices, patens, crosses, candlesticks – and churches were left with bare essentials. Vestments of satin or velvet went also. Chantries and guilds were closed down. Details of the Bedford confiscations have not survived, but from all the Bedford churches they must have been much more numerous than those at Luton parish church, which we know included two silver chalices and patens, a silver cross, and blue velvet vestment and cope.

THE PROPERTY MARKET

The confiscation of the property of religious houses resulted in a great redistribution of land. This is most obvious in the country-side, since all of them had scattered estates of greater or lesser extent, but it also affected the town. While much was retained in the king's own hand, much also was sold, and was sometimes bought by speculators who sold to others, so that there was a period of unusual fluidity.

The actual site of a monastic house usually passed to a gentle-man who used it for a home, with more or less adaptation accor-ding to his means and preferences. What was left of Newnham was leased from 1559 as a residence by Sir Robert Catlin, chief justice of the Queen's Bench; but much of the stone, especially of its church, seems to have been taken soon after the Dissolution to Willington for new farm buildings (now property of the National Trust) by John Gostwick, who had been one of the commission-ers concerned with the closing down of both Newnham Priory and the Franciscan friary. The residue left at Newnham was eventually pulled down. Elstow Abbey became the home of Sir Humphrey Radcliffe, and was rebuilt as a house early in the next century by his successors, the Hillersdons. In Bedford itself, much of the Franciscan friary building remained till this century. At Caldwell a surviving stone cottage probably incorporates frag-mentary remains of the priory's outbuildings.

Much property in Bedford town changed hands, since not only did several Bedfordshire religious houses own property in Bedford (chapter 3), but also some outside the county, such as Bermondsey. The most considerable holding was that of Newnham Priory.[5] In the built-up area its annual rents exceeded £40 (nearly as much as the prior's pension), while its agricultural land in the open fields was more than 400 acres.

One Bedfordian who turned the situation to account was John Williams alias Scott, mayor 1546, 1549 and 1551. In November 1545 he paid £254 for a large amount of ex-monastic property, which seems to include practically the whole Bedford property of Bedfordshire religious houses.[6] There were six houses belonging to Harrold Priory, five to Elstow Abbey, four to Warden Abbey, eight to Chicksands Priory, eleven to Caldwell Priory, and no less than thirty-two holdings of houses or land belonging to Newnham Priory. All the tenants' names are given, and often the streets – High Street, Well Street, the Shambles, the Poultrymarket, Potter Street, Rygge Street, Colles lane are all mentioned. The *George* inn is included, and also the schoolhouse occupied by Robert Hill (probably the schoolmaster). Many of these may have been insignificant cottages and tiny amounts of land; one item is a barn; but even so, it was a considerable transaction for a local businessman to carry through before the days of banks. The date of the grant is near Williams' mayoralty; could he have been acting for an unofficial consortium of burgesses?

Probably wherever practicable the properties were sold off to the occupiers; and where this was not practicable to others. We do not find a Williams 'empire' in later Bedford, though we do find a Williams concerned in property wrangles a century later.[7]

SIDE-EFFECTS

It was at this stage that some side-effects of recent changes began to appear. The bridge deteriorated because there was no chaplain there to receive alms for its upkeep, and so no repairs were done. The walls decayed so much that it was said there was danger of children and cattle falling into the river.

A temporary expedient was found by using stone from St Peter Dunstable as it was pulled down, and reserving twenty loads for future needs. But some permanent machinery was needed, and by 1569 bridgewardens were appointed.

Then there was the school. Apparently the old schoolmaster (Robert Hill?) carried on, but what was to happen when he died? and how long would the new owner of the building (Williams) be willing to make it available for teaching purposes? The school may have been attended by Williams himself as a lad; he did not want to close it, and had a door sent there from St Peter Dunstable as it needed a new one; but he did not propose to saddle himself with much expense. On the other hand, William Harper or Harpur, perhaps his former schoolfellow, was now doing very well in London, a member of the Merchant Taylors' Company, and soon to become alderman; moreover Harpur had no children.

Perhaps Williams and Harpur talked the matter over. In 1548 a new schoolmaster, Edmund Green, came from New College, Oxford, and it seems very probable that Harpur paid the stipend. Then Harpur went further, and bought (perhaps from Williams) a site near St Paul's church on the land which had belonged to the dissolved Trinity guild, and here he built a new schoolhouse (leaving Williams free to dispose of the old one!). As yet he made no permanent endowment; perhaps he still hoped for an heir. But the canny Williams, once more mayor, obtained in 1552 letters patent from Edward VI authorising the corporation to accept an endowment for the school if such were forthcoming. The climax came when Harpur, Lord Mayor of London in 1561, bought 13 acres 3 roods of farmland in Holborn, and in 1566 conveyed it to the corporation as an endowment for the school.

In all this the important figure is that son of Bedford, William Harpur.[8] We get glimpses of him during his mayoralty of London: presiding at the Lord Mayor's show (a pageant showing harpers, mythical and historical, of all ages), joining in Christmas festivities, foxhunting, inspecting London's water supply, patrolling the city at night (at the age of 65) when disorder threatened, and helping with the provision of armed men for overseas service.

Though Harpur was attached to the town of his birth, he was wise enough to see that it was inadvisable to trust Bedford business-men with the appointment of a schoolmaster. This responsibility was given to New College, Oxford.

In the background of the whole affair, we glimpse that astute Bedfordian, John Williams.

Local initiative had coped with two of the problems left by recent changes. A third needed national legislation: the problem of the poor. This naturally was not caused by the disappearance of monastic alms, but it was intensified by it. The closure of the religious houses happened at a time when there was less employ-ment in the countryside. An increase in sheep-farming, and some enclosure for this purpose, meant that fewer men were required. The gradual disappearance of the old ties of serfdom allowed men to leave the village more easily. It was in the town that such men would hope to find opportunity. Then, though the church had always stressed the duty of giving to the poor, and many testators did so, perhaps there was emerging very slowly a feeling of public responsibility.

This feeling of responsibility appears in Harpur's endowment of the school. Should there be a surplus from the income from rent of the Holborn property, after payment of the schoolmaster and usher, and repairs of the schoolhouse, that surplus was to be applied to the marriage of poor maids and to alms for the poor.

The emergence of public policy was slow. Between 1536 and 1572 legislation and Prayer Book rubrics increasingly tried to stimulate almsgiving by providing almsboxes in church and instituting collectors. Nominally, almsgiving was still voluntary, but an element of compulsion was growing. But it became clear that this was not sufficient. Finally by a law of 1597 (reissued in 1601) it became obligatory for each parish to appoint overseers of the poor, who would levy a parish rate, and apply this to the apprenticing of poor children, provision of work for the able-bodied, and relief of the old.

Thus each Bedford parish had to appoint parishioners who (supervised by the justices of the peace) would carry out this duty. (Incidentally, though the exact date is not known, Bedford at some time before the reign of Elizabeth I obtained its own commission of the peace, so Bedford overseers would be supervised by Bedford justices, not by county ones).

Already in 1555 parishes had been directed to appoint surveyors of the highways, who would direct repair work on roads within the parish. Thus in the parishes civil machinery emerged, complementing the ecclesiastical side represented by church-wardens. In a country parish, it was simple in operation, as the civil parish officers dealt with the community as a unit. But in Bedford, because of the number of parishes, there were complications. On the one hand was the municipal machinery: mayor, bailiffs, chamberlains, bridgewardens, constables; on the other, a kind of infrastructure in the various parishes, dealing with roads and poor relief in their areas.

It is unfortunate that in Bedford parishes only a limited number of records have survived, so that we cannot trace the working of parish machinery at all thoroughly. Naturally, St Paul's was the most important, but their overseers' records survive only from 1763, while for surveyors there is a single document of 1788. For

St John, overseers' accounts survive from 1698; St Mary, 1832; St Cuthbert and St Peter, which in any case were outlying rural areas, not at all. In the town the overseers of the poor certainly functioned; but the system of parish road repair did not work out so well; and later we find measures about this emanating from the municipal machinery.

In Bedford the county justices set up a house of correction, where vagabonds could be put to work. The first reference to its site in High Street is in 1629.[9]

A DEVELOPING TOWN

A growing town needed more trading facilities, and in 1554 the grant of an additional market, to be held on Tuesday, was obtained.[10] There was dissension about where this was to be held. In 1557 two country gentlemen who acted as arbitrators (Nicholas Luke and Humphrey Radcliffe) decided in favour of south of the river, where the space left vacant opposite St Mary's church by pulling down that of St Peter Dunstable offered a convenient site. Here also was held a second fair, with cattle tied to the railings of nearby houses. Within a few years shops were built nearby. The Saturday market continued to be held in High Street.

More thought began to be given to the town's administration. The burgesses bethought themselves that, centuries previously in their first surviving charter, they had been bidden to model their arrangements on those of Oxford. So in 1556 various questions were addressed to Oxford: how far did the mayor's responsibilities go? Who fixed court days? What was the bailiffs' function?

THE BLACK BOOK

From 1562 more careful note was kept of rules laid down. These rules or 'constitutions' were made at the court leet, (just as in a village agricultural rules were made at the manor court). At the court leet, others besides the burgesses were present, though the initiative was usually taken by the burgess jury. From 1562 till 1603 these 'constitutions' were entered in the so-called Black Book.[11] They may not be complete, and it does not seem that the book was always kept systematically, but they do give some picture of Elizabethan Bedford.

The mayor, and the two bailiffs (the oldest officers) were elected annually by and from the burgesses. Refusal to serve involved a £10 fine. They took office at Michaelmas, when the mayor gave a dinner to burgesses, while it was the responsibility of the bailiffs to entertain 'all commoners and foreigners'. The bailiffs were to keep their wassail 'as of old ancient time'. If, as suggested earlier (chapter 4) this was connected with the collection of the hagable, its interruption may be due to the fact that the hagable, like all fixed rents, had declined in value and so in importance. At all events, the old custom of wassail was now re-affirmed.

At the feast of St Thomas the Apostle, the chamberlains and the bridgewardens presented their accounts. These officers seem to have been appointed by the other burgesses at a meeting of the 'Hall' or 'Council Chamber', which was the forerunner of the later Town Council (the merchant guild being presumably now moribund or obsolete). The 'Hall' was attended by all burgesses, who must wear their gowns, unless they wanted to pay a fine of 2s 6d. Seemly behaviour was expected at this assembly, and no one should speak 'malicious or unseemly words', or 'lay his hands upon his weapon'.

Both mayor and bailiffs had serjeants. When the mayor went to church for divine service, his serjeant, also gowned, must walk before him with the mace, the symbol of office. The serjeants were at this time putting in for a rise; they felt that their wages of a penny a week and 6s 8d at Christmas were inadequate, and their stipends were increased to 20s pa.

Besides presiding at the meeting of the 'Hall', the mayor sat beside the recorder at the court leet.

The status of burgessdom is defined in the Black Book. A register of burgesses was kept. When a burgess had a son, he reported at the next meeting of the court leet 'the name of such man child as God shall send him', and it was added to the register on payment of 2d. If a 'foreigner' applied to be a burgess, he must have within the town goods and chattles to the value of 40s, to make sure he would be able to pay his dues; for instance, he must pay his quota towards renewing the charter when appropriate.

It did not as yet seem necessary to define the freemen, who were the most active of those townsmen who were not burgesses. Practically the only right in municipal affairs which they had was to appoint three representatives to join with three aldermen and six burgesses on an assessment committee when levies had to be made (for instance, when paying the expenses of the town's MPs). In 1597 there was a proposal at the court leet that they should be allowed to share in electing mayor and bailiffs, but it came to nothing. As yet, their place in municipal affairs was held to be rather one of owing duties than of having rights. It was their duty to discharge humble offices such as bucket-searcher and constable.

The wards are distinguished by name from about 1590. North of the river were High Street East, High Street West, Well Street, Prebend, St Loyes or All Hallows, St Peter, St Cuthbert, Mill Lane. South of the river were High Street (ie, St Mary), Potter Street (Cardington Road), Caldwell Street, St John.

TRADE
The Black Book also gives some trade regulations. For tanning, the place for selling raw hides was limited to 'nigh unto the well in High Street', or 'under St Mary's churchyard', ie, near the two market places. Tallow candles might not be made in any house near High Street. As regards the strength of ale, brewers must brew 12 gallons for every quarter (peck) of malt. Incidentally, at this time people of substance still brewed their own beer, as did tavern-keepers. Brewing for sale was in its infancy, and only two 'common brewers' at this time are known: Samuel Christy and Simon Beckett, both of whom were presented at the court leet in 1588 and 1597 for not selling at the regulation price of 1d a quart.

Bakers must sell thirteen loaves to the dozen. Butchers actually did their slaughtering in the Butcher Row or Shambles, at its nether end. They were directed to clear away the 'inwards and entrails' daily, so as not to annoy neighbouring inhabitants 'with any corrupt savour or smell', but they only took this refuse as far as Offal Lane (now Tavistock Street). They were allowed a fortnight for handing on the fatty parts of slaughtered animals to the chandlers. Fishers must not use nets.

Prices of victuals were fixed by the mayor. Breach of this rule meant a fine of 3s 4d, or even imprisonment in the noisome Stonehouse (or after 1589 in the former chapel on the bridge).

No reference is made to pillow lace, but it is probable that lace was beginning to be made in Bedford in this period. From what we know elsewhere, it was probably made at home by poor children, whose instruction was arranged by the overseers of the poor, especially in St Paul's parish; so there would be no occasion for mention of it in municipal records.

No one could set up in business in the town without first approaching the mayor, who would consult with the other officers and with the burgesses. If the proposal came from an apprentice, who had served seven years in the town, consent would be given, subject to his presenting to the Hall or Council a gallon of wine. If this was not the case, the Council would consider 'whether the party be a meet man to occupy in the town or no'; and if so, what he must pay for the privilege. A currier who set up without permission was presented at the court leet in 1593.

Market rules are given. On market day, the bell for commencement was rung at 11 o'clock, probably to allow plenty of time for the arrival of country folk. These must pay toll; for grain, this was 2d for four quarters or $\frac{1}{2}$ peck of grain; for other goods, $\frac{1}{2}$ pint for four bushels. Butchers from elsewhere had their 'standings' below those of Bedford butchers, and they must only sell their hides and tallow 'to tanners, glovers and chandlers of this borough'.

FARMING

Farming practices are regulated by the constitutions in the Black Book, since it was still the case that many townsmen were engaged in agriculture, either full or part-time. In fact, it was one of the mayor's duties to approve a municipal herdsman, an honest man. Each morning, at three successive places, this herdsman blew his horn, and townsmen brought their cattle to him for him to take them to pasture until evening. Then, on similar summons, they came to collect their cattle and take them home for the night. For this service they paid the herdsman $\frac{1}{2}$d weekly for each beast.

The right of pasture was rationed. The allowance was one cow, ox, or bullock, and one horse, for every 20 acres. Thus evidently the right was exercised only by well-to-do townsmen.

It was easier to keep sheep, for the allowance was one sheep per acre. Easiest of all was to keep a pig, for these were not rationed. However the swineherd or 'hoggerd', who was appointed by the mayor, had to be paid. Also townsmen must not let their pigs wander in the streets, and must keep them ringed. One bull and one boar for the use of the whole town were kept 'according to the old custom' by the farmer of the Bury Farm. A bitch in heat must be kept at home.

Even for farming, burgesses had special rights. There was Burgess Land (34 acres in Newnham Field) and Burgess Mead. Apparently these were for the use of burgesses who had served the office of bailiff.

PUBLIC HEALTH

As yet, there were few rules about public health and safety. One prime danger was that of fire. Now that tiles were becoming generally available, a rule was made that existing thatched roofs must be covered with tiles or slates. Faggots might not be piled within 10 feet of any chimney, and the mayor appointed two wood-searchers to see that this was observed. The keeping clean of Butcher Row has already been mentioned. The river banks must be scoured by those who lived nearby. There was a fine of 20s for throwing dung or carrion into the Ouse.

From other sources we get evidence on epidemics. Burial registers show that in 1574–76 about thirty people died of the plague in St Peter's parish. In St Paul's parish two years later the chamberlains distributed £10 'to the people of this town in the time of God's visitation of sickness'.

THE COURTS

The records of the town courts, where they survive, show the kind of disputes that came up. There were three courts: the borough court of quarter sessions (a recent addition): the court leet for minor offences, and where also rules or 'constitutions' were made; and the court of pleas for civil cases. Slander, driving away another man's cattle, selling an unsound horse, using false dice at cards, stealing a purse or a cloak – these are the cases that come up. A debt is not repaid – the security might be a feather bed or a silver goblet, and the sum involved as little as 4s. A poor witch, Agnes Jeffes, in 1591 was imprisoned for a year, and thereafter had to stand six hours in the pillory; eventually, when a third case was brought against her in 1594, she was hanged.

Cases like this indicate a harsh society, as indeed Elizabethan society was. Indeed, one of the so-called improvements of mayor Williams was to make 'a large and pleasant place to bait bull and bear', instead of the old cramped site next to St Paul's church, behind the high altar.

In 1605 a notorious highwayman, Gamaliel Ratsey, was hanged at Bedford. His last exploit had been to take £174 from a horseman near the town. He prolonged his last speech to the assembled crowd till a storm broke – 'so that he could see them all well washed'.

HOUSEHOLDS AND SHOPS

Domestic inventories for the Elizabethan period are rare in Bedford, but one survives for 1588 for Thomas Edwards. He was fairly well-to-do. His hall or living-room was hung with painted cloths, and contained table, form, chair, cupboard, four cushions, and three old coffers. He had two bedsteads, with sheets, pillows and bolster. In his kitchen were three kettles (or cauldrons), two pots, and a frying-pan. His utensils were of pewter. His wardrobe included two doublets, one of leather and one of canvas, and two pairs of hose, one russet, one frieze.

Wills give clues to the distribution of trades. There were those who prepared clothing materials – weavers, dyers and fullers; and those who sold them or made them up – mercers, drapers and tailors. A surviving tailor's bill for 1592 charges 20d for making a jerkin, the cloth costing 8d, buttons 3d, and taffeta for trimming 6d; while one for making gowns in 1597 charges 1d for hooks and eyes (these gowns were of black, trimmed with lace and velvet). Gloves and shoes were then made locally; in 1592 a glover, Richard Pearce, was presented at the court leet for washing his limed skins in the river.

Also practising in the town were pewterers, who made household utensils; at least one potter; cutlers, saddlers, smiths, coopers and joiners. Concerned with building were masons, tilers, carpenters and painters. One tiler who was due to appear at the court leet in 1588 was marched off to Tilbury in the Armada scare, so his fine for non-appearance was waived.

THE TURN OF THE CENTURY

The century drew to a close. Harpur died in 1573; his burial in

St Paul's church was something of an occasion, when the chamberlains provided three gallons of Gascon wine and a gallon of sack.[12] The churches had new plate: (St Paul, St Mary and St Cuthbert all have chalices and patens dating from 1569–70), for there was now a conscious effort, after the loss and confusion of earlier years, to build a positive Anglican church. The archdeacon probably had a drive in preparation for the bishop's visitation of 1573, when the corporation on four occasions sent him either wine or sack, at a total cost of 7s 8d. Indeed, some of the clergy were willing to go further than was countenanced by the new Anglicanism, and were developing views of their own on simplicity in worship. In 1578 it was reported to the archdeacon that the rector of St John's did not wear a surplice; and the same was said of the vicar of St Peter's at the bishop's visitation in 1585. At St Paul's, the vicar, Ralph Jones, seems also to have puritan tendencies, for there was dispute in 1581–82 between him and the mayor, Alexander Hunt, who insisted on having St Paul's bells rung 'immoderately' on saints' days. The next vicar, Andrew Dennis, was one of a small group of local clergy who met in a Puritan 'exercise' – a whole day's session consisting of lesson, psalms and sermons.

Can we imagine the outlook of older townsfolk in Elizabethan times? Perhaps older Bedfordians can do so, for we have seen our Bedford change from a quiet little town with horse-drawn traffic, where we knew the shopkeepers, to one that is large and important, with vastly improved facilities for libraries and hospitals, but has lost an intimate quality that we prized.

An Elizabethan Bedfordian might recall how at one time as he walked over the bridge he would have a friendly word with the chaplain, and now the chapel was a lock-up. If he turned into a church to say a brief prayer, he might think the whitewashed walls cold, after the former bright pictures; and when he went to church on Sunday there would be no coloured vestments, perhaps not even a surplice.

If on a summer evening he walked by the river to Newnham, that great and imposing pile of buildings was gone – as Shakespeare said, 'sometime lofty towers I see down razed'. If he was in distress, there was no kindly almoner; the parish overseer looked him up and down, and if he did not tell the applicant that he was a nuisance to the parish, clearly he thought so. Bedford was larger and was thriving – the elderly townsman may have thought to himself – but it was not the town of his youth.

5 NOTES

Hist. Beds., 194–200.
1. *B.H.R.S.*, xxv, 23, 25, 79.
2. *V.C.H.*, i, 356.
3. *Hist. Beds.*, 187, 193.
4. *Linc. Rec. Soc.*, liii, 88, 91.
5. *B.H.R.S.*, xxv, 15–81.
6. *L.P. Hen. VIII*, xx, pt. 2, p. 446.
7. *B.H.R.S.*, xxvi, 111.
8. *Harpur Trust*, 5–6.
9. *B.H.R.S.*, lvi, 42.
10. *B.H.R.S.*, xxxvi, 13.
11. *B.H.R.S.*, xxxvi, 20–37.
12. *B.H.R.S.*, xxxvi, 29.

6   Puritanism and Civil War, 1603–60

If the 16th century was eventful, the next sixty years were still more so. In this thriving town some were hoping to develop trade further by a new method. But trade and profit are not the only influence in human affairs; another is the struggle for power, and this struggle was about to explode on a national scale. Moreover there was to be one on a smaller scale in Bedford itself. And intertwined with both was that independence of spirit, that questioning of authority, to which the general availability of the Bible had given a strong impetus.

RIVER NAVIGATION

A century of stable government had given Bedford the chance to reach its full potentiality, in existing conditions, as a centre for the northern two-thirds of the county (Luton and Leighton catering for the southern remainder). Further development, apart from natural growth, could only be by improved communications to reach a wider area. Though the roads were now comparatively safe, they were impeded by mud in wet weather and ruts in dry periods; and they varied every few miles according to the efficiency (or lack of it) of the parish surveyor. But what of communication by water?[1] Centuries ago invaders had come up the river. True, there was now the complication of water-mills every few miles, and the local miller had his own need for water. Moreover, some stretches were overgrown, and others were uneven in depth, so that there would need to be much clearance, and also some device for controlling the flow. Towing-paths would be required for the horses who would tow the barges or lighters.

Could all these difficulties be surmounted, what an impetus for Bedford! In particular, it would mean that coal, brought by sea from Newcastle to King's Lynn and so called sea-coal, could be brought up the river to Bedford. Not only would this be an advantage to Bedfordians; Bedford could act as clearing-house for the supply of coal over a wide area. This was important, since wood for fuel was becoming ever scarcer, as more land had been taken into use for agriculture or pasture. On their passage downstream to fetch the coal, the lighters could carry Bedfordshire produce.

The possibilities of river navigation in general in grandiose, if hazy, terms seem to have occurred first to a Middlesex man who in 1617 obtained from the crown letters patent giving him the right for 21 years to make rivers navigable; he was to pay £2 per annum, and could keep what profits he made. This venture was a general speculation, for he soon (1618) assigned his rights in the Ouse to a Cople man, Arnold Spencer, and his London associate. Spencer's partner withdrew, but work had been begun in Huntingdonshire, where six sluices were built.

The sluice or stanch was a forerunner of the lock. A lock has gates at either end, and the water within the lock is raised or lowered to facilitate transfer to a higher or lower level of the river, as the case may be. The older method provided only one gate 'for penning up or raising a head of water and letting down the same'. When it was closed, the level of water above was raised; on opening, there was a rush of water down which boats could ride, or up which they could be hauled with the help of a line or winch.

Much work and expense must have been involved in making the Huntingdonshire sluices. Not surprisingly there was dissension over the amount of toll which ought to be paid at each. Traders thought that a penny a ton was sufficient. The Privy Council consulted the county quarter sessions of both Huntingdonshire and Bedfordshire, and they favoured 3d a ton. Still disputes continued. Thus Bedford traders, who may have been already getting coal through the Huntingdonshire sluices as far as St Neots and then overland, knew what was going on. They realised that comparatively little was required to get passage from St Neots to Bedford and open up a clear way from Bedford to the sea. And though the scheme had not originated with them, they were anxious to push it.

Chief among them was the mayor, Steven Luxford. Arnold Spencer wanted to continue the work. Perhaps an act of parliament would help. A large and apparently enthusiastic council on 30 April 1628 declared themselves willing to bear the expense of promoting such an act 'for so great, good and laudable a work'. The sluices were to be built by Spencer, who would be entitled to a toll of 2d a ton. The certificate was signed by 66 burgesses, among them representatives of prominent families, such as Beckett, Eston and Hawes. It states that the signatories know that 'great profit will redound to the said town'. Spencer noted on the certificate 'received from Mr Mayor'.

The project for an act came to nothing. Charles I's breach with parliament was coming to a head; he dissolved it in March 1629, and did not call it again for eleven years. However, Spencer obtained from the king by letters patent a grant for a further period, and Luxford helped him with the first sluice at Eaton Socon. In the course of the 1630s the navigation reached Great Barford. Here were set up near the bridge 'shops, conveniences and yards . . . to lay coals and salt and other commodities' brought in lighters, so that Great Barford became temporarily a depot pending the remaining work required to reach Bedford. The end seemed in sight, though Spencer was already heavily in debt. Then in 1640 Charles I was again driven to summon a parliament. The Civil War was on the way, and for twenty years the national power struggle held up all efforts such as the Ouse navigation.

POWER STRUGGLE: NATIONAL

The confrontation which was forming in the early 17th century was between the monarchy and parliament. The House of Commons consisted almost entirely of country gentry, since all over the country, as in Bedford, boroughs were sending gentry as their representatives. It had become accepted that taxation was authorised by parliament. At first taxes tended to be levied only in special circumstances, and consent was automatic. Now, frequent taxation was unavoidable. The commons began to feel that they were in a position to make conditions. Of the minority who tended to support the monarchy, one was Richard Taylor of Clapham, deputy recorder for Bedford.[2] (Incidentally, it may be convenient to note here that the position of recorder was becoming an honorific title to be bestowed on an aristocrat or other important person, who would be a patron to the borough; while

E

the actual work of legal advice in court cases was given by a deputy.) Taylor was also one of the borough members of parliament in 1620, 1623, 1625 and 1628.

When Charles I, harassed by the Commons' attitude, called no parliament for eleven years, and in order to build up the navy levied taxes (ship money) on his own authority alone, opposition began to build up. Bedfordshire in 1635 was required to provide £3,000, of which Bedford's share was £120 (Luton £40, Leighton £48). For the first year, the sheriff managed to collect it, but in 1637 the number of defaulters was growing. When in 1640 the king, driven to do so by other difficulties, again called a parliament, Richard Taylor lost his seat.

One of the earliest election documents to survive for Bedford is one for this election. It is a list headed 'Good voices (votes) for Sir Samuel Luke', a keen parliamentarian. Among his supporters are John Eston and Robert Hawes; while the families of Beckett and Faldo would have supported the more moderate candidate, Sir William Boteler.

In 1642 war broke out. Bedford was now affected by, and to some extent involved in a struggle with which probably most inhabitants felt little concern. This involvement took three forms. There were the decisions emanating from the parliamentary authority, the Committee of Both Kingdoms, and from the local committee in touch with it. There were the occasional military flutters which occurred in an outlying area on the fringe of the main struggle. And there was the interruption to individual lives and to the town's trade.

By parliamentary ordinance the county was associated with seven others in the Midland Association. A Bedfordshire committee was set up, consisting mainly of country gentry. Townsmen however were soon involved, such as John Neale and Dr Francis Banister, and of course the mayor for the time being.[3] This committee was mainly concerned with raising forces (from 400 to 600 in the county each year) and money. One regiment was raised by Sir Samuel Luke.

The military activity in Bedford was small. By parliamentary authority a fort was set up on the old castle mound, and walls erected with loopholes for shooting. Its garrison of about a hundred was commanded by Captain Benjamin Hudson, who conscripted from the surrounding villages the labour required. Cromwell passed through Bedford in 1644 and 1645, with 600 horse and dragoons. These troops used St John's church, and the churchwardens' accounts show payments 'for making clean the church when the camp was here'. Later the same year 300 royalist horse came through Bedford, and there was fighting on the bridge.

Bedfordians were less than enthusiastic about having the war at close hand. Some petitioned parliament to dismantle the fort and make Bedford an open town – John Eston called these the 'ill-affected'. However, that autumn, by order of the parliamentary command, the fort was sleighted, and Captain Hudson was transferred to Leicester.

Since the main royalist area was to the west, the outlying defence for Bedford as for the county was Newport Pagnell. Here in 1643 Sir Samuel Luke, who had distinguished himself in battle, and had also acted as scoutmaster for the collection of information, was made commander. Here in 1644 he fought off a royalist attack. His letter-book shows his many difficulties over inadequate supplies and forces.[4]

And finally there was the interruption to individual lives. There were those like Samuel Gibbs who, in the middle of their apprenticeship, either volunteered or were drafted into the parliamentary army, and after the conclusion of their war service found difficulty in 'setting up' in trade in Bedford. Others served in the garrison at Newport Pagnell.

POWER STRUGGLE: LOCAL

If to most Bedfordians both the battles and the aims of the Civil War seemed remote, more were concerned with the power struggle in Bedford itself between the burgesses and the freemen, which had showed its first stirring as long ago as 1425. It had stirred again in the 16th century, just as did independence in religious thought. The uncertain times of the Commonwealth offered opportunity.

The burgesses were the prosperous men. They held the municipal offices and attended the council. Such were Robert Hawes (d. 1628), owner of Duck Mill, whose daughters were married to gentry, and who was able in his will to leave £10 to Bedford poor; also Simon Beckett the brewer, more than once mayor; William Faldo, glover; and John Eston.

The freemen and commoners were the great majority. They could only attend the court leet, and hold inferior offices such as wood-searcher, constable, or bucket-keeper (this office was set up in 1612 to check that inhabitants had set out leather buckets of water in case of fire); and they could act as parish overseer. Their economic status varied from modest comfort to a bare subsistence level.[5] An example of the former is the mason, John Brown. His household equipment included two tables, a form, a chair, two cushions, four stools, and a cupboard; in his kitchen were spit, gridiron and pothanger; in his two bedrooms were two bedsteads, three chests, a flock bed, sheets and pillows; while his utensils included eleven pieces of pewter, two brass pots, and three little candlesticks. The extreme of poverty is represented by another John Brown, whose only goods worth mentioning were a blanket, a hammer and a hobbing iron.

The more thoughtful (and no doubt also the more substantial) of the freemen asserted themselves at the court leet, and in 1610 they secured the right to have thirteen representatives on the council. It is not clear that these representatives were themselves freemen, nor did the new arrangement take effect at once, but only as vacancies arose.

When the Civil War was won, and a feeling of change was in the air, in 1647 the freemen demanded annual elections. The angry dispute was referred to three representatives from each side; one of the burgess representatives was William Faldo, grocer; and one of the freemen Thomas Gibbs, cooper. The burgesses stood firm. Then the freemen petitioned parliament. The burgesses counter-petitioned: if freemen could hold municipal offices, who would be left to be constables and bucket-keepers? But the climate of the time was with the freemen. In 1650 a parliamentary committee approved annual elections and a larger council.

That same year the climax of the struggle was reached. The new council abolished the distinction between burgess and freeman. Though in several towns at this time a similar struggle was proceeding, only High Wycombe and Bedford got so far.[6] However, the great majority of humbler folk in Bedford knew little of all this and cared less.

It is about this time (1647) that regular council minute-books began to be kept, and these give more details of the municipality.[7] It was in 1647 that William Scott became the town clerk, and he seems to have been a town resident. Previous town clerks had lived as far away as Podington (William Payne, d. 1624) and Sharnbrook (John Cobbe). Such distant residence had been practicable because the town clerk only acted occasionally when called in to do so, and charged fees for what he did. Centuries were to elapse before the emergence of a full-time town clerk. But already it was seen that there was some advantage in choosing one easily accessible.

An ordinance of July 1649 deals with 'repairing and cleansing the common streets'. 'For taking away all ambiguity', it was laid down that the bridge was the responsibility of the bridgewardens; High Street, including St Mary's and by the guildhall, from ridge to gutters came under the chamberlains; but from gutter to house or shop was the responsibility of the occupier, as were all other streets. Repairs on all were to be carried out by October.

The occupants of premises in High Street were also obliged to provide street lighting. This resolution is headed 'For setting forth lights in the night'. On alternate nights the east and west sides of High Street, from the *Peacock* inn in St Peter's parish to the way to Ampthill in St John's parish, were to set out 'a candle-light of the bigness at least of sixteen in the lb to be kept burning, and renewed as it is spent', from dusk until 8 am.

In 1648 a bedell of beggars was appointed, whose duty was to arrest travelling beggars, and to whip them when ordered to do so. His wages were $\frac{1}{4}$d monthly from each householder assessed to the poor rate. We find references to a pesthouse in St Loyes for use in epidemics such as the plague; at other times it was let.

The council had also to deal with problems of the school's endowment. The London land system was to let on long leases. The tenant who by 1626 seems to be leasing the whole property (which was in four separate plots), under an agreement which would terminate in 1652, was William Langhorne. But before his death he sublet to others. Perambulations had not been made, and boundaries had become uncertain. Since the time for a new long lease was approaching, the council in 1649 applied to Chancery for a commission to investigate. Two surveyors twice measured the land, but were unable to reconcile the conflicting claims. The solution was to effect an exchange, so that each claimant's area would be in a solid block instead of scattered.[8] This was ratified by Chancery decree in 1654. Meanwhile four members of the council were having complicated negotiations with the existing occupiers, preparatory to arranging a new long lease – negotiations which dragged out for years.

The navigation was not entirely lost sight of.[9] In 1650 the council asked the recorder (Sir Samuel Browne, a judge who had bought Arlesey manor) to petition parliament for an act to promote it, and urged this again in 1653. But the times were not propitious.

A reference in 1647 to the town lock-up on the bridge (the former chapel) shows that at this time the house adjoining, normally occupied by one of the sergeants-at-mace, had been taken over by his widow's second husband, who 'withholdeth the same from the bailiffs . . . and for want of a convenient prison divers felons have escaped'.[10] The offender, Richard Mabbott, was to enter into contract with the bailiffs to guard prisoners.

INDEPENDENCE IN RELIGION

Both nationally and locally the demands for greater scope and responsibility had been intermingled with that independence in religious thought apparent in the last century. If a king could differ from a pope, why could not a subject differ from both king and archbishop? And if he so differed, why could he not join with others who were like-minded? The accessibility of the Bible to the growing number who could read gave a powerful impetus in this direction. This was happening all over Bedfordshire.

On the other hand, the Anglican policy of trying to develop a seemly and decorous worship based on the Prayer Book and on an ordered hierarchy had also zealous adherents. In Bedford the most notable was Giles Thorne, a rector of St Mary's, and also there was Theodore Crowley of St John's. The Civil War and Commonwealth threatened those whose religious sympathies and political loyalties inclined them to the royalist side. Thorne was arrested as he came out of the pulpit by Lord St John's troops, and carried to the Fleet prison, where he remained five years without trial. He was replaced by a 'godly and painful' (painstaking) minister, Thomas Holden.

For independent thought the climate was now favourable.[11] There were already in Bedford 'godly persons, zealous to edify themselves and to propagate the gospel, keeping always a door open and a table furnished and free' for like-minded ministers, though they were as yet unorganised. Chief among these were John Grew and John Eston senior, both aldermen, and Anthony Harrington who was elected to the enlarged council. In 1650 they took the formal step of constituting themselves an Independent congregation. Such congregations were emerging elsewhere during the Commonwealth. In Bedford the immediate cause was the discovery of a minister to their mind, John Gifford, who had come to Bedford a few years since.

This remarkable man had, oddly enough, formerly been an officer in the royalist army, and had led a rakish and gambling life till he underwent a conversion. After some heavy losses at play, while in desperate mood, he chanced to look into a religious book, and this meant for him a turning-point. After a month in 'a great sense of sin', he seemed to discover 'the light of God's countenance', and forthwith sought the company of the little group mentioned above. In spite of their initial distrust, he persevered patiently time and again. Eager to share his newfound conviction, he persuaded them to give him a chance to preach, at first privately, then publicly. After several meetings for prayer and guidance, the little group were completely won over. They formally became a congregation with him as their minister. The living of St John's, in the corporation's gift, being vacant by sequestration, and the Independent element on the council so strong, in 1653 John Gifford was presented to the vacancy, and henceforth the congregation met in St John's church.

It is an indirect testimony to the strength of the Independent church that Quakers, who during this period gained a widespread following in the rest of the county, and even held a national meeting at Beckerings Park, made no headway in Bedford. (Not till 1931 did Bedford have a Quaker meeting'.)[12]

The strength of the Independent element on the council shows the interrelation of an independent religious spirit and a policy of change in municipal affairs.[13] The list of church members includes certainly other members of the council, Edward Covington, Richard Spencely and possibly John Spencer, while surnames occurring on both are Fenn, Norton, Edwards, Gibbs, Hawkins and Wells. Six of these were among the seven petitioners to parliament for a reformed council in 1649, and four were spokesmen for the freemen at a conference in January 1650; while two (Alderman Grew and John Spencer) were among the four spokesmen of the corporation. When the new council of eighteen was elected in March, eight were known members or likely associates of the congregation.

A decisive moment came in 1655. Gifford died, leaving to his followers a long epistle of love, advice, and exhortation for the future, ending 'Walk in love one to another . . . search the Scriptures . . . stand fast'.[14] A congregation so zealous and active naturally expected to choose his successor, such right being an essential part of their new-found freedom from the Anglican hierarchy. But in the view of more conservative members of the corporation, if what had happened exceptionally in Gifford's case were now allowed to repeat itself, a further precedent would have been set up; and a piece of valuable town property – the advowson – would be on the way to being lost to the corporation. This time apparently the council acted before the congregation had come to a conclusion, and in September presented William Hayes of Papworth.[15] The congregation appealed to Cromwell, who, after giving audience to both parties, decided for them. The Commonwealth register of ecclesiastical appointments records on 16 January 1656 that the presentment to St John's of John Burton, nominated by His Highness Oliver, Lord Protector, is approved by the commissioners for approving public preachers.[16]

Two months later (19 March) Simon Beckett, mayor, and four members of the council were removed from office by Cromwell's major-general for the area.[17] It is not clear beyond doubt that the dispute over St John's, now settled, was the actual cause of this action, but the dispute is clearly part of the trend of affairs leading up to it. The new mayor was John Grew, and the new council members included John Spencer, Richard Spencely, and Thomas Gibbs.[18] In August the major-general himself was admitted.

The Commonwealth drew to an uneasy close, with the death of Cromwell and a period of uncertainty.

6 NOTES

Hist. Beds., 257–65.
1. *B.H.R.S.*, xxiv.
2. *B.H.R.S.*, xxv, 104–9.
3. *B.H.R.S.*, xviii, 3.
4. *B.H.R.S.*, xlii.
5. *B.H.R.S.*, xx, 86, 112.
6. P. Clark and P. Slack, *English towns in transition*, 1500–1700, 137.
7. *B.H.R.S.*, xxvi.
8. *Harpur Trust*, 9.
9. *B.H.R.S.*, xxvi, 38, 73.
10. *B.H.R.S.*, lvi, 17.
11. *B.H.R.S.*, lv, 15.
12. Mr Gilmore tells me that there was admitted in 1744 a Quaker freeman, George Chalkley Taylor, the corporation having previously taken legal opinion as to whether a Quaker could be admitted, since he would not take the oath of allegiance but only affirm. However, George Chalkley Taylor was non-resident (he lived for a time at Maulden and was a member of Ampthill Friends' Meeting), but he was an unsatisfactory character, and was disowned by the Friends in 1765.
13. *B.H.R.S.*, xxvi, introduction pp. xxxii–xxxiii.
14. *B.H.R.S.*, lv, 18–21.
15. J. Brown, *John Bunyan*, 97–8.
16. *B.H.R.S.*, xxvi, 91, 93, 96.
17. *B.H.R.S.*, xxvi, 95.
18. *B.H.R.S.*, xxvi, 99.

7   Reaction and Renewal, 1660–1700

The restoration of the monarchy was like the breaking of a log jam when the ice melts. Frustrations had been building up, with no clear way ahead. Now, though slowly at first, the former pattern began to be resumed – but with a difference. The twenty-year recession gave place to a revival of trade, and work on the river navigation was renewed, with all its possibilities for Bedford. The burgesses largely recovered their dominance of the corporation. The Anglican church once more took the lead – but Independence could not be suppressed.

RELIGION

To take religion first: what happened in Bedford must be seen against the national background. The drive towards a restored Anglicanism came partly from parliament, partly from the Anglican hierarchy; it was welcomed by some and accepted by most. The new parliament passed acts restoring ejected ministers to their livings (Giles Thorne returned to St Mary's); excluding from corporations all who refused to take the Anglican sacrament (1661); and re-authorising the Prayer Book (1662). In Bedfordshire a new archdeacon was appointed in 1662, and archdeacon's court-books from that year show a new activity. Then, as it became clear that the new policy was not universally accepted, in 1663 a Conventicle Act forbade non-Anglican worship; and in 1665 the Five-Mile Act forbade an Independent minister to come within five miles of where he had served.

For Bedford Independents an important event happened some miles from Bedford, and to a member who had only recently come to live in the town. This was the arrest in November 1660 at Harlington of John Bunyan. It was at the outset of the new reign, and before the national policy had taken legislative form. It was the outcome of local initiative acting on an almost forgotten act of the previous century.

Anglican opinion in the archdeaconry generally had suffered mounting frustration. When Dr William Foster of Bedford and his brother-in-law Francis Wingate of Harlington (a county justice of the peace) heard that John Bunyan was coming to Harlington to preach, they decided to act under an old Elizabethan law. From Bunyan's own account of their talk with him, it is clear that they hoped to frighten a rising young man, and send him home with a word of caution. But they were attempting more than they knew. Before many years had passed, it would become apparent that Bunyan was Gifford's most notable convert, and he himself would emerge as of national stature, indeed of international stature.

A brasier from Elstow, Bunyan apparently served in the parliamentary garrison at Newport Pagnell. After discharge from the army, he was occasionally in Bedford in the course of his trade. Himself a seeker, he chanced in 1653 to overhear the conversation of some women Independents. 'Methought they spoke as if joy did make them speak . . . they were to me as if they had found a new world.' As a result of this meeting, Gifford, now living in St John's rectory adjoining the church, invited the young man to come and talk with him, and Bunyan joined the congregation. Those conversations were later recalled by Bunyan when he wrote of the pilgrim Christian being helped at the Interpreter's house.

Soon Bunyan (who had moved into Bedford into a house in St Cuthbert's Street) began to accompany members of the congregation when they went preaching in the villages, and it became realised that he had a special gift for talking to ordinary folk. Now, in November 1660, he was faced with the choice of capitulating to authority, or of standing firm and awaiting trial by quarter sessions, with all the difficulties condemnation would cause for his four children and his young second wife. He stood firm. He was sentenced to be imprisoned until he conformed. For twelve years he remained in the county gaol at the corner of Silver Street and High Street. His young wife succeeded in getting access at the *Swan* inn to the Assize judge when he came round, hoping that the judge could override county quarter sessions, but without avail.

Meanwhile the Independent congregation, ejected from St John's church, met in each other's houses, in spite of sporadic attempts to suppress them. In 1670 at John Fenn's house, where

Nehemiah Cox was speaking, the congregation was arrested in a body. Heavy fines were imposed, which were not paid. The resulting distraints led to uproarious scenes. Spectators hooted at the officers distraining, and when the objects collected were directed to be taken to an inn yard, the innkeeper refused access. A brass kettle belonging to Edward Covington was left in the middle of the street. It seems clear that there was in Bedford much sympathy for the congregation.

Such sympathy grew as Bunyan (in between supporting his family by making many thousand gross of long tagged laces) began to write. His spiritual autobiography, *Grace Abounding*, appeared in 1666, and he began work on *The Pilgrim's Progress*. In 1672 Charles II's attempted intervention on the side of moderation brought about his release. He was now officially pastor of the Independent congregation.

One more attempt was made upon him. He was prosecuted in the archdeacon's court for not taking the Anglican sacrament at St Cuthbert's church, and was excommunicated. This had as consequence imprisonment by the sheriff's order in the county gaol. Here he completed *The Pilgrim's Progress* (part 1) before his release, which took place when two Londoners stood surety for him.

Before his death in 1688, he wrote a number of other works, but it was *The Pilgrim's Progress* which went into edition after editon, and began to be translated into European languages.

The position of the Independent congregation at Bedford had changed. Thirty years previously it both had a good moral standing and was also active in municipal affairs. Now its members were debarred from municipal activity, but its moral standing was enhanced by the reputation of its most famous member.

In 1689 the Toleration Act was passed, which allowed nonconformist congregations, provided that their place of worship was registered with quarter sessions or with the archdeacon. The Independents had in 1672 bought a barn and part of an orchard in Mill Lane from Josiah Ruffhead. On this site a permanent building was erected in 1707.

THE CORPORATION

Meanwhile, what had happened to the corporation? Here again, the conservative burgesses, feeling themselves in a strong position, acted before the national policy had time to take shape.

The first change was the reduction of the council to thirteen; this was passed on 29 August 1660. These thirteen members were to be chosen from a list of 26 nominated by 'the mayor's house', ie, 'mayor, aldermen and bailiffs, towndwellers'; and the election would be made by 'the rest of the commonalty'. This ambiguous wording shows that the conservatives already had in mind reviving the distinction between burgesses and freemen, which in fact they spelt out on 31 October 1661. On 19 August 1663 they went further, and laid down that nominees for the council must be burgesses.[1] Thus the final outcome of the disputes of the 17th century was that freemen had the right to elect annually, from a list of nominees supplied by the burgesses, the thirteen burgesses who formed the council. It was not much, but it was something. The method of election was by word of mouth. The clerk read the list, and 'noted the number of voices' for each candidate.[2]

The council had closed in on itself. By national legislation it had lost those active and concerned Independent members of the previous decade, whose presence must have contributed to cross-fertilisation. By its own action it had retreated to almost the same socially restrictive position of former years.

It did, however, at first maintain links with the county family of St John of Bletsoe, who had been active parliamentarians. In 1661 it appointed the Earl of Bolingbroke as recorder. Paulet St John was one of the borough MPs. But in the 1680s government intervened once more. Pressure was put on boroughs generally to renew their charters, for the practice of obtaining a new charter from each successive monarch had lapsed. Such pressure may have given Bunyan the idea for his *Holy War*, 1682, in which the town of Mansoul is attacked by Diabolus. In Bedford's new charter of 1684 the royalist and conservative Earl of Ailesbury of Houghton House was appointed recorder, in place of Lord St John.

THE SCHOOL ENDOWMENT

In this year of the new charter, another matter came to a head: that of the school endowment.[3] At first, things had gone well with the management of the contiguous area allotted under the Chancery decree of 1654. In 1668 a 41-year lease was made with a single tenant, William Thompson, who was to pay an improved rent of

£99 per annum. The great fire of London in 1666 set off a train of rebuilding and development, which began to reach the hitherto agricultural area of Holborn. One active developer was Nicholas Barbon, who persuaded the existing tenant, Thompson, to assign his lease (which would expire in 1709) to him. He then secured from the corporation in 1684 a further lease to take effect 1709–60. For this latter period he was to pay £150 per annum.

To secure these concessions Barbon paid £250 down. A fine on the renewal of a lease was customary, but £250 was more than twice as much as Thompson had paid when obtaining his lease. Moreover, in future the endowment income would do more than pay the modest salaries of master and usher and the repair of the school; there would be some balance for the charitable payments which were to be made when a surplus arose. In point of fact, Barbon's schemes were rather more grandiose than he could effect. When he died in 1698 his affairs were in confusion, and his lease of the Harpur endowment went to mortgagees. But the development of Holborn, with all its promise for the future, had begun.

However, in 1684 all this was in the future. The £250 fine which Barbon paid seemed to the corporation to come very opportunely. The cost of a new charter had always been levied on the burgesses, but this was something that had not happened for a long time. Moreover, the cost was high; with the expenses incurred by the mayor, Paul Cobb, in London while negotiating it, the total came to £144 – a good deal more than the £100 tax the burgesses had voted.

Was the fine trust income? Or was it a perquisite? Cases are known elsewhere much later than this of such fines being treated as perquisites. When the accounts were presented (somewhat late – January 1686) the council took the view that the fine was a perquisite and not part of charity income. The new mayor, William Faldo, said 'I do protest against the allowing of any of the money given or coming to the town for charitable purposes to any other use or purpose'. He was outvoted.[4] Had it been the council of thirty years since, with Independents and freemen, would he have had more support?

RENEWED INTERVENTION

That pressure from the government which Bedford had already

experienced in the compulsory appointment of a new recorder in 1684 was to go further under James II. The Stuarts, though accepting that they must summon parliaments, were feeling their way in other directions to stretch their power if possible. The new king hoped to promote general tolerance, and thus to help Roman Catholics. At Bedford in 1688 he removed the mayor, Thomas Underwood, and six council members, including William Faldo and Robert Beckett, and replaced them with his nominees.[5] This was in line with similar action elsewhere. The result was general opposition throughout the country. Soon James II was in exile, and the throne offered to William and Mary. Henceforward no more such pressure was to come from the monarchy to Bedford.

Boroughs generally had changed a good deal from the medieval interplay of local initiative and royal grant. The trend now was for those in power to retain their privileges, rather than to develop experimentally. At the same time a step towards uniformity through national legislation had been taken.

THE NAVIGATION COMPLETED

Hopes for the navigation revived, as trade began to recover.[6] The help of the recorder (at the restoration the Earl of Bolingbroke) was sought. At long last an act was passed in 1664/5 for making navigable divers rivers, including the Ouse. The corporation in gratitude resolved to entertain the recorder with a collation, of which the cost was not to exceed £10.

However, the act of itself achieved nothing till someone should be prepared actually to undertake the work for the final stretch from Great Barford to Bedford. In fact, for want of scouring, the river seems to have somewhat silted up between Eaton Socon and Great Barford. These works and those further down the river were the responsibility of Spencer's heirs, the Jemmatts. In the last resort, the act empowered the county justices of the peace to appoint an undertaker, and Henry Ashley of Eynesbury was prepared to act. Some county justices as landowners were doubtful of the project; not so however the Earl of Bolingbroke, who in 1680/1 was himself engaging in coastal trade from Newcastle with his ship, the St John.

The new recorder appointed in 1684, the Earl of Ailesbury, was approached by all parties. He came to the conclusion that bringing boats to Bedford would benefit town and county generally. Thomas Christie, MP (for once Bedford was represented by an attorney from the town) did his best. At last in March 1687 the county justices appointed Ashley undertaker. Ashley acted expeditiously, and the work was completed by September 1689. A legal battle ensued between Ashley and the Jemmatts as to their respective rights to the tolls. But as far as Bedford was concerned, the aim had been achieved. The arrival of the first lighters must have been an occasion.

Gradually there developed at Bedford an extensive trade, with cargoes coming up river for distribution, and others being despatched down river. Riverside sites (some previously tanyards) began to be bought up for coal yards, especially between the bridge and Batts ford. Among the burgesses concerned were William Beckett (mayor 1675, 1683, 1689), William Isaack (mayor 1687–8) and Richard Chicheley, who in 1696 was bringing 700 chaldrons annually up the river. William Faldo (mayor 1697, 1711) was supplying Wrest Park with coal.

These merchants did not own lighters or barges, but hired watermen, mainly from St Neots and St Ives, paying them a freight charge. At this date the lighters were small, and covered with a hair cloth or tilt. They travelled in gangs of nine or ten. The horses on the towpath who pulled them were led by boys of eight years old and upwards, who in summer slept in the fields by their charges.

The cargoes up river included fish, mainly after 1695. These were brought in holed trunks towed behind the barges. (Celia Fiennes in 1701–3 noted that riverside Bedfordians kept their fish fresh in such trunks). The main merchant here was the fishmonger, John Tompson, who was dead by 1715. Other cargoes were salt, millstones, tar, bricks, iron and deals.

Down river went agricultural crops (wheat, oats, barley, peas, beans and apples); and also malt and fuller's earth.

THE TOWN IN GENERAL

In 1671 we get a bird's eye view of the town from the returns of the short-lived hearth tax, a tax which necessitated the listing of inhabitants with the number of hearths per householder.[7] Those in receipt of poor relief were exempt, but their number; given; and those too poor to be assessed to pay poor rat listed by name, but without details of their hearths (probably those in this category had only one hearth).

From these returns, the population of Bedford has been calculated as 2,130: St Paul, 1,140; St Mary, 395; St Peter, 217; St Cuthbert, 212; St John, 166. There seem to have been rather more than 500 houses in Bedford. Those householders receiving poor relief numbered 56; while 74 were too poor to be assessed for the poor rate. Even of those who did pay poor rates, about a hundred had only one hearth. Thus nearly half the population were very poor.

Of those townsmen who were more comfortably off, 73 had two hearths; nearly 200 had three or four hearths; while 44 had five hearths and over. In this last group are Thomas Christie, the MP and attorney, with no fewer than twelve hearths in his house in Mill Lane. William Foster in the Prebend ward had nine hearths. Dr Thorne in Caldwell Street had six. Merchants like William Faldo and the Becketts appear also in this category, and the Independent John Eston.

The current names of the wards were: (St Paul) High Street east, High Street west, Prebend, Well Street, Mill Lane, St Loyes; (St Mary) High Street, Potter Street, Caldwell Street; while St Peter, St Cuthbert and St John each constituted a ward.

It was about this time (1667) that a town scavenger was appointed at £3 per annum. In this century bridge repairs were the responsibility of the chamberlains, who in summer when the water was low, went out in a boat to inspect the pillars, and were allowed for their dinners 12d and also the cost of the boat.[8]

During this century we get some more lasting attempts by well-to-do townsmen to help their poorer neighbours.[9] Sometimes a charitable endowment was for the whole town; other testators felt particular responsibility for those of their own parish. The objects varied. Thomas Hawes, who died in 1688, left money for the regular provision of bread. A specific group, such as widows, might be mentioned: Ann Collins (by birth a Hawes) in 1682 left a bequest for ten poor widows; and much earlier, in St Paul's parish, Jonas Andrews had left money for widows. Mary Paradine in 1631 left money to provide coats, shoes and stockings for old men. A more substantial bequest was that of that active Bedfordian, Thomas Christie, whose will in 1697 provided for eight almshouses for unmarried poor.

For this period some unusually full Assize records have survived, which give details of local crime.[10] Among the Bedford cases is the theft of a horse in 1682 from an innkeeper's stable: the latter (Humphrey Shelton) deposed that when he came down in the morning, a grey horse was gone from his stable, together with a saddle belonging to one of his guests, and the yard was littered with straw which had evidently been put down to deaden the sound. Another case concerns a theft from the market: Valentine Curby, a stallholder, lost from his stall a box containing bone lace, cravats and linen.

The issue of counterfeit money in the town in 1679–80 provides a number of documents. Some time previously (during and just after the Commonwealth) there had been a shortage of coinage, and many traders issued tokens inscribed with their names which they would honour against future purchases. Bedford traders who did so include William Faldo, William Isaac, Ralph Smith, linendraper, and one or two innkeepers. However, this shortage had now been remedied. The counterfeiting gang included Valentine Hallowfield, a saltstone maker from Gloucester, and on search his lodging was found to contain whiting and a mould frame; while more whiting was found in the house of a mason, Richard Robinson.

Other cases at assizes at this time include one of alleged witchcraft: John Wright, a cordwainer, 'being demanded whether he was a witch, saith he did not know, but trust to God he is not'. Violence also occurs. In 1668 there was a death following a drunken brawl. An old tanner, Samuel Lane, thrust his way into an alehouse in St Mary's one evening, and called for drink. Soon afterwards the goodwife, who had left the room, heard a noise and returned; she found the candle out (apparently there was only one), and Lane bleeding.

By now plague was slowly dying out. In 1637 there was an isolated case: Mistress Paradine (perhaps wife of Thomas, mayor 1634) brought it back from London;[11] a Bedford surgeon named Rowland was called in, and consultation had with a physician of county reputation, John Symcotts, but she died. As late as 1655 forty persons north of the river died of the plague.

It was in 1678 that the first post office was set up in Bedford at the *Swan* inn, collection being made three times a week. Previously the nearest post offices were at St Albans, Little Brickhill or Huntingdon.

In 1672 a freak storm hit Bedford. Inn gates were blown off at the *Swan* and at two other inns; two houses in Offal Lane were blown down, and a tree was 'carried over Paul's steeple as if it had been a bundle of feathers'.

7 NOTES

Hist. Beds., 257–65.

1. *B.H.R.S.*, xxvi, 138, 149, 174.
2. *B.H.R.S.*, xxvi, 139.
3. *Harpur Trust*, 11–13.
4. *Harpur Trust*, 12.
5. Corporation minutes 1664–88, f. 290–1.
6. For this section, see *Lock Gate*, ii, supplement 4–18.
7. *B.H.R.S.*, xvi, 144–9.
8. *Lock Gate*, i, 3.
9. *V.C.H.*, iii, 31–3.
10. C.R.O., H.S.A.
11. *B.H.R.S.*, xxxi, 62.

8   The Eighteenth Century

The eighteenth century saw still further development of Bedford as a trading centre; a turning-point in the expansion of the school's endowment income, with all the consequences of this for education in Bedford; a new attempt to use Bedford in a political power struggle; and still another religious movement. At the end of the century the surviving overseers' records for the largest parish (St Paul) show how the parochial system of relief was working.

A TRADING CENTRE

Now that the river was navigable up to Bedford, waterborne trade increased rapidly. For this period, some of the toll-books survive for that half-share which went to Spencer's descendants (the Francklins of Great Barford). Their accounts show takings of £548 in 1741, £1,038 in 1760, and £1,701 in 1790.[1]

The most valuable single cargo coming up river was coal. Coal wharves extended along the riverside at Bedford. Sometimes successive merchants can be traced for a period, as on the north bank near Batts ford.[2] Here, at the beginning of the century Thomas Battison had a wharf. At his death in 1732 his estate amounted to nearly £41,000. The wharf was inherited first by his son Robert; then by his daughters. They let it to William Theed, another coal merchant, who later (1775) purchased the messuage, wharf, coal yard, landing-places and 'great stable'. Incidentally it was customary at this time for a Bedford merchant to act as county treasurer, and William Theed held this office for 43 years (1750–93). Another coal merchant nearby, William Watkins, extended his property in 1789 and 1792.

The toll-books give some indication of the quantity of coal brought up by one merchant. Round about 1730 the biggest importer was Thomas Wilkes, who between June and September had 800–900 loads. As to the total amount leaving Bedford at this time, some of the coal merchants (William Faldo, Thomas Wilkes, Thomas Battison and Joseph Barnes) estimated it in a letter of 1729 to an influential country gentleman, John Orlebar of Hinwick, as 5,000 waggons annually.[3]

Such loads were a heavy addition to traffic on the surrounding roads. The upkeep of these depended on the inhabitants of each successive parish through which they passed, and these inhabitants (who in any case looked on road work as a tiresome duty) had no incentive to increase their work for the benefit of through traffic.

Something more was needed. This came in the form of a toll to be collected on the road as on the river, so that the cost of upkeep would fall on users. At intervals gates would be set up, with a small cottage for a toll-keeper. The whole was managed by a group of trustees, usually country gentlemen, appointed by act of parliament.

The system developed piecemeal. There was no overall plan: gradually here and there, as public interest was energetic, turnpike trusts were set up for particular stretches of road. The first in the county was some miles from Bedford. Then in 1727 and 1754 came the trust for the Luton–Bedford–Rushden road. In spite of the advantage their traffic would derive, the coal merchants' initial reaction was annoyance that so much of the cost would fall on them, and they were highly incensed when a tollgate was set up on the outskirts of Bedford. In 1757 a trust was set up for the road from Bedford to Hitchin. One from Bedford via Willington to the Great North Road followed in 1772; to Woburn in 1777; and to Kimbolton in 1795. On the other hand, there were difficulties about the road to Northampton; an act was passed in 1754, but was ineffective; and this road had to wait till 1814.

These improved main roads perhaps did something to hold down the cost of cartage. The Bletchley parson, William Cole, whose coal came from Bedford, complained in his diary of its high cost in 1766 (ie, before the road to Woburn was turnpiked); he tried to eke out coal with cow dung.

Another trade which was expanding in Bedford was that of brewing. Whereas at one time beer had been brewed by many people, frequently for their own consumption, a trend increased for a brewing firm to expand, and to sell beer over an area, especially to inns. Brewers also favoured riverside sites, both for despatch of beer, and for intake of barley and malt. One such brewer whose business was growing was Thomas Woodward. His brewery was beside the river, with a road entrance from St Paul's Square.

The domestic craft of making pillow lace in fine point-ground was now well established for women and girls in Bedford, as in the villages of north and west Bedfordshire, Buckinghamshire and Northamptonshire. It helped to swell the income of poorer families. A craft of this kind leaves little written evidence, but a key factor was the laceman, who provided patterns and thread, and marketed the finished product. In Bedford two such are known: James Matthew, 1725, and Isaac Hayes, mayor 1742.[4]

The market was still held in High Street. In the late 17th century, a markethouse had been built in the middle of the street, the upper room being converted in 1705 for use at assizes. But the obstruction to traffic proved increasingly vexatious, and the markethouse was pulled down in 1780.

THE CORPORATION

The main pattern of town government continued as established after the restoration: a council of thirteen, elected by freemen from a list of twenty-six nominees supplied by the aldermen. The aldermen were also kept to a total of thirteen. The mayor and bailiffs were during this period elected by the freemen from a list of six nominees, three names being supplied by the aldermen and three by the council. Thus there was very little opening for the admission of new men to any position of responsibility.

The town clerk, still only part-time, was now usually resident in the town. An unusual town clerk in this period was Matthew Priaulx. He arrived in Bedford as New College's nominee for master at the free school in 1718, when the corporation was disputing the college's right to appoint; and he finished up as town clerk.

On the town council, there were two ways in which the chance of change could be enhanced. If an alderman died or left the town, the next mayor would be chosen from outside the ranks of aldermen, to keep the number at thirteen. Should more than one alderman die, there was greater opening for agitation.

The other method of promoting change or of influencing elections to parliament was by creating new freemen. Hitherto a freeman was generally the son of a freeman, or one who had served apprenticehsip in the town. Now new freemen were frequently created on payment of a guinea fee. The class struggle of the previous century was now dormant. Division was mainly on party political lines (Whig and Tory). Whatever party might be in power did not scruple to create freemen to improve their voting strength at an election. It was also possible to induce ex-Bedfordians who had left the town to return to vote at an election.

The diarist Benjamin Rogers, Bedford born (son of a vintner) and rector of Carlton, took a great interest in these matters, and would ride in from his country rectory to get the news. Thus in the 1731 mayoral election, the Tories engineered the return of several distant freemen, with the result that their candidate, Thomas Cave (also the aldermen's nominee) polled 182 votes as against his opponent's 74. 'It was wonderful to see so many Tories come to town upon the election morning from all quarters, even Lincolnshire and Essex'. The new council followed a similar pattern.

The most famous creation of new freemen was to take place some years later in 1769. To assess that, it is necessary first to follow the borough's reaction to outside influence in the shape of intervention by the Dukes of Bedford.

POWER STRUGGLE

During this century Bedford was again affected by the national power struggle, but in a different way. The day of baronial retainers and of parliamentary armies had passed; it was clear that the country was to be governed by a combination of king and parliament. But there are other ways of gaining power and influence than by force: what of wealth? A new aristocracy had grown up, whose estates were expanding. In Bedfordshire there were the Russells at Woburn, newly created Dukes of Bedford, and gradually buying land in the county as opportunity offered. The Russell wealth was increasing, since by marriage they had obtained a large area in Bloomsbury, which was now developing. Successive Dukes had political ambitions, and tried to influence the elections not only of the two county MPs but also of the two for the borough.

The first efforts in this direction were made by the third Duke. This took the form of outright bribery; he declared that he knew the election of 1727 was to be bought, and he would buy it, even at the cost of four guineas a vote. Blatant bribery, however, endangered its aim; the election was followed by a petition, as a result of which one of the Duke's men, James Metcalf, had one seat, while John Orlebar had the other. Metcalf's death resulted in a by-election in 1731; this time the Duke had oxen killed and beef distributed. The corporation determined to resist pressure, and one wrote at the time that, if necessary, they would create new burgesses and new freemen. Benjamin Rogers writes in his diary of all the manoeuvrings, and adds 'there was the greatest appearance of noblemen and gentlemen that was ever known at any elections'.[5] The result was that the Duke's man lost by 31 votes (the total number of votes cast being 719, ie 375:344).

More subtle were the methods used by John, 4th Duke of Bedford, who succeeded in 1732 at the age of 21, and lived till 1771. His plans matured over the years. He hoped to attain to the position of recorder – ie, to be the borough's acknowledged noble patron. He began to buy up property in Bedford. Between 1749 and 1761 he made eleven purchases, some of them extensive. They included St Leonard's farm in the south of the town, three houses in High Street, several in St Peter's parish, other property in Ford Street and in Bendhouse lane, and three inns, the *Bear and Dog*, the *Rose*, and the *Peacock*. (Ultimately the Russells obtained and rebuilt the *Swan*, but the chance for this did not come till 1787).

In 1752 he was helpful over the question of a sessions house. The old guildhall near St Paul's church, consisting simply of a hall or upper floor above butchers' shops, had long been thought by county justices to be inadequate for quarter sessions, and they usually met at the *Swan*, but meeting at an inn also had drawbacks. A new and larger public building or sessions house on a more extensive site seemed indicated. A site was chosen on the south of the square, formerly the site of the *Castle* inn, and the money was to be raised by public subscription, both from town and county. The 169 subscriptions ranged from county aristocracy and gentry, one or two of whom were able to afford as much as £100, down to modest Bedfordians who subscribed 10s. The Duke advanced 500 guineas, made the purchase, and then conveyed the site to eighteen county justices and four borough justices, in trust to be used for assizes, for town and county quarter sessions, and for Bedford petty sessions. Among the trustees was always to be the Duke's heir in possession of Woburn Abbey. The four borough justices were William Theed, Charles Jackson, William Edwards and Robert Butcher. The last name is significant: it was that of the Duke's agent-in-chief.

Correspondence which has recently come to light shows that as early as the 1740s Butcher was actively in communication with a number of Bedfordians.[6] Hence it may well be that the Duke's influence is behind the events which preceded the falling-in in 1760 of the lease of the Holborn property given by Harpur, and which led to a drastic change in its management.

This management of what was becoming an important area on the fringe of London, and of its greatly increased financial return were such as would challenge the competence and integrity of any borough at that time. Already the burgesses of Bedford had a reputation for treating themselves in London when they went up to perambulate the estate: much later, Goldsmith says in *She Stoops to Conquer* 'Sir, do you think we have brought down . . . the corporation of Bedford to eat up such a supper?' How then would things be when the income was much increased? The Duke's London house and his Bloomsbury estate were a short distance from the Harpur property, and he was thus aware of the financial prospect ahead.

In Bedford itself the corporation's record of management in the early 18th century was not promising. There was inevitably tension in the partnership by which the Free School was run, with New College appointing master and usher, and the corporation controlling the endowment. The latter tried to 'oversee the school', and in 1718 to appoint the master, till New College by legal action forced them to give way. On the other hand, they would not raise the teaching staff's salaries. In 1739 New College appointed a master who received the salaries of both master and usher. The number of boys at the school sank to eleven in 1747.

It was at this stage that the corporation was challenged as to its administration of the charity. Some townsmen were willing to act. The Independent, Thomas Woodward, whose brewery adjoined the school, Francis Jennings, another Independent, and others brought a successful case in Chancery in 1747. The Lord Chancellor in giving judgement directed that, on expiry in 1760 of the existing lease, a new scheme of administration should be submitted to him. In 1761 a Chancery decree appointed a holding committee consisting of the Duke, his heir, his agent, and two country gentlemen, and also appointed a receiver.

For the negotiations which followed during the interim period, the Duke's agent, Robert Butcher, was largely responsible. He sometimes lost patience, and once wrote to the Duke that the burgesses were 'insolent and treacherous'. But at last all was agreed; 'they submit all to your Grace', and in 1764 an act of parliament removed full responsibility for the school and endowment from the corporation, and transferred it to a new body, the Harpur Trust (see below).

The Duke's policy was showing returns. At the 1754 election, the two MPs, R. H. Ongley and Francis Herne, were agreed on between Duke and borough. In 1761 his brother-in-law, Richard Vernon, was one of the representatives. And in 1767, on the death of Lord St John, the Duke became recorder of Bedford.

So powerful a patron, however, would not, if active, long find willing compliance. Already at the 1768 election there was opposition to the Duke's candidate – 'an utter stranger; a head seems to be making against the Duke's interest'. The seat was won by Samuel Whitbread of Cardington, owner of a London brewery; and he sat as one of the borough representatives till 1790.

In 1769, during the mayoralty of John Heaven (he was of Holborn origin, and had been admitted as a freeman in 1759, becoming council man and burgess in 1767) the record total of 500 freemen were admitted – known as guinea-pigs from their guinea fee. Many were from outside the county, especially from Huntingdonshire. When the Duke died in 1771, the corporation chose as next recorder a Huntingdonshire whig, Sir Robert Barnard, who might be counted on to be helpful, but was not influential enough to be dominant.

The corporation had not allowed themselves to become subservient to one of the most powerful and wealthy figures in contemporary politics. But their reckless creation of non-resident freemen distorted the pattern of election in Bedford for years to come. At the 1790 election, only 1,058 votes came from townsmen, while 736 (of whom 146 were from Huntingdonshire) came from elsewhere.

THE PARISH SYSTEM

The Harpur Trust set up in 1764 to administer Harpur's endowment worked by a combination of the corporation and the parishes. Thus it is advisable first to consider the parishes. Since Tudor times, the parish had secular functions. To most of the humbler townsmen the parish was the authority which primarily concerned them. This applied also to poor nonconformists, since, though they were probably helped by their co-religionists, it was from the parish overseer that they would obtain statutory relief. Bunyan's granddaughter, Hannah, died supported by St Paul's parish in 1770.

Guided by the census of 1801, we may postulate in the late 18th century a population of a little over 3,000. Of this, half would be in St Paul's parish, one-sixth in St Mary's, with smaller numbers in St Peter, St Cuthbert and St John. In each parish the overseers must make a rate, to be levied on all those able to pay. It was usually collected in four instalments. From its proceeds they must make payments to those in need: usually to the old and the sick, apprenticed orphan children, and (in a large parish) run the workhouse. At the Easter vestry meeting, they presented their accounts to be approved by other parishioners, and by two borough justices (of whom usually the mayor was one). In 1771 St Paul's overseers accounted for upwards of £600.

One preoccupation of the overseers was to prevent poor people from outside the town gaining a settlement in Bedford, and so becoming eligible for relief there. Such people were removed to their place of origin by justice's order. In 1778 five were so removed from St Paul's: to Thaxted, Thomas Stock and his wife Susanna; to Holborn, Dorcas Rogers; to Millbrook, John Dimmock; to Pavenham, Martha Baseley; while Ann Grant and her daughter were removed to St Peter's parish in Bedford itself. On the other hand in this year an equal number of people were returned to St Paul's from elsewhere: from Hitchin, John Bailiss;

91

from Riseley, Thomas Goss and his wife; from Northill, Hannah Browning and her child; from Eggington, Mary Stiles and child; and from Holborn, Mary Rushton and child.

Sometimes examination before a justice gives details of the life of some of these wanderers. Thus in 1783 we have the evidence of Edward Jackins. Born at Thurleigh, at first he worked for various farmers. Then he got a job in St Paul's parish with William Franklin, brewer, and this he held for six years. After that he went wandering to Pavenham, to Eynesbury, to Harrold; and then he got a job at the *Saracen's Head* in Stonehouse Lane in St Paul's parish. He had a wife and seven children.

Military service sometimes appears in these accounts. Thus George Sissons, of Lincolnshire origin, served in the 14th Foot, and married Ann Whitehouse of St Paul's.

An inventory of St Paul's workhouse in 1772 shows that there were 23 beds, of which each had a blanket, with a rug or coverlet, and most had a bolster; but only 18 pairs of sheets are listed, of which at the time the inventory was taken three were 'in wash'. There were a few chests and coffers, two long dining tables, 25 chairs and some stools. Another inventory of 1769 lists the cooking equipment as two brass kettles, two brass pots, two saucepans (one of them old), a frying pan, dough trough and pickling tub.

THE HARPUR TRUST

The setting up of the Trust[7] meant that the corporation no longer had sole control of a matter of importance to the town: of the Harpur bequest, its school or schools, and its welfare payments. Yet for the first thirty years the corporation was, so to speak, let down lightly: the 1764 act set up a partnership between it and the parishes.

The corporation's officers were to be trustees: mayor, recorder, bailiffs and chamberlains; so also were the 13 aldermen and the 13 members of the council. With them, however, were to act the ministers of the five parishes and representatives of those parishes. If everyone attended, the number would be between forty and fifty persons; but in practice attendance was usually between ten and twenty. There was a professional clerk in Bedford; and in London there was a receiver to deal with the estate.

It was clear that the corporate trustees would have the main influence. Aldermen such as Gidney Phillips, John Cawne, and

William Parker were the most frequent attenders. The parish representatives came seldom and seem usually to have been over-awed; while the clergy scarcely appeared at all.

The trustees' interests were varied. A few professional men seem to have been anxious to forward the grammar school, partly on account of their sons, for Greek and Latin were necessary for a university or professional career. Smaller tradesmen thought of education in terms of reading, writing and arithmetic; and also were concerned to see that contracts for work for the Trust were fairly shared out. The humblest were chiefly interested in welfare payments.

In this period the grammar school was put on a better footing. The Tudor schoolhouse was repaired and re-fronted, with a statue of Harpur in 18th century dress. Arrangements were made for St Paul's bell to ring to summon the boys to school. The grammar school boys assembled on the upper floor of the school-house. A new house for the master, with wainscoted study and parlour, cost £800 (the work being shared out in 13 lots so as to be fair to local tradesmen). Later a semi-detached house was built for the usher. But improved salaries and housing did not of them-selves ensure able staff and a growing school. The time of expan-sion was not yet.

Provision was also made for more modest education. On the lower floor of the school house was established a 'writing school', where were installed five desks and nine forms, bought 'as cheap as possible'. The hours were: 9–4 in winter 7–5 in summer. The writing master lived next door to the usher.

With the increased income, Harpur's residuary provisions for welfare could take effect. It was a pity that these were not in some respects re-thought. In Harpur's time a policy of statutory care for the poor was only in process of being worked out, but now a parish system of poor relief had been working since 1597. Again, in Harpur's day, education for girls was a rarity; now it was in some places being promoted by enlightened benefactors. The 1764 act however did not venture to depart far from Harpur's original stipulations. What the Trust did under this act was to supplement the work of parish overseers, and, as regards girls, to supply them, not with education, but with marriage portions of £20 obtainable by lot.

93

For the young generally, both boys and girls, there was help with apprenticeship (again obtained by lot). For homeless or orphaned poor children, a residential home was opened in a converted house in what is now Harpur Street in 1773, with thirty children. For the old there was 'hall money', a cash distribution on St Thomas' day. This had begun on a very small scale towards the end of the corporation's management – £37 being distributed in 1751; but now it was on a larger scale. Compiling the list of those eligible (poor decayed householders who had lived in Bedford for five years) posed problems.

There was now strict accounting, with expense scales laid down, and accounts printed annually.

RELIGION

After the struggles of the 17th century, how had religion fared in this growing and changing Bedford? The early part of the 18th century was a time of quiet co-existence. The Anglican church went on its even way. At intervals the Bishop of Lincoln came on visitation: in 1706 Bishop William Wake was at Bedford, where representatives of the four northern rural deaneries waited on him; 'our confirmation was large and everything done in great order' he noted in his diary. He stayed with the archdeacon, Thomas Frank, who was rector of Cranfield, and the vicar of St Paul's, Alexander Leith, dined with him. The archdeacon's court still continued to function, sitting in St Paul's church, though it was of diminishing effect. Among the Bedford cases which came before it was one of defamation of Mary Bunker in St Peter's parish in 1732; Sarah Bodington of St Paul's was ordered in 1751 to do penance for having a bastard child; and Joseph Willis of St Cuthbert's was in trouble over non-payment of church rates in 1770. We know that some townsmen at least were committed Christians; Thomas Pierson, a grocer, born in 1712, was taught by his grandfather to pray morning and evening; and when he was confirmed 'I was deeply concerned how I might give myself to God'. During this century music gradually came back into use in church services. St Paul's church installed an organ; the salary of the organist, William Weale (£20 p.a.) was paid by the corporation, and he composed a tune called 'Bedford'.

To the Independent meeting in their new building in Mill

Street came not only many Bedfordians, but also country folk from many villages round. This was partly because only a large congregation could afford to pay a minister. At first such ministers, like Ebenezer Chandler (1690–1747) had no training, as they could not go to university; but gradually nonconformist colleges were set up, and Samuel Sanderson (1747–66) was trained at a Yorkshire academy and also in London. Some of the distant members of the Independent meeting began to find the journey too much; and those at Gamlingay set up their own church in 1710, Blunham following suit in 1724. At Bedford singing was allowed on the Lord's day from 1697. Here also the congregation kept watch over the lives of its members: thus Brother Butcher was reproved for Maypole dancing and card-playing in 1702; Sister Bell was suspended from communion in 1757 for back-biting; and drunkenness was one of the offences for which Joseph Negus was 'cast out' in 1756.

One question vexed the meeting in the course of the century: should baptism be allowed to infants or only to those reaching years of discretion? The meeting's practice had always been flexible on this point, but Sanderson's successor, Joshua Symonds, in 1772 told his congregation that he had come to believe only in adult baptism; yet he did not resign his post. An uneasy period of attempted compromise followed; till a group consisting among others of Ann Belsham (daughter of Thomas Woodward) felt obliged to secede from what now became known as the Old Meeting, and set up a New Meeting a few yards further along Mill Street. One member who felt bound to support them was as yet unknown: a Cardington man, who also had a house in Bedford which he occupied on Sunday to facilitate attendance at meeting: John Howard.

It might be thought there would not be room for another religious movement in Bedford, but this century showed that there was. Stability in church matters seems to bring with it, at least for some, a falling-off, and a blunting of perception. Religion cannot be accepted at secondhand; its price is eternal vigilance. And the new breath, when it comes, almost inevitably has some difference in form.

First came the Moravians. This movement, stressing the need for life lived fully in the spirit of Christ, had spread from Germany to London, and thence to Bedford. Two Anglican clergy of London, being invited down by Jacob Rogers, curate of St Paul's, and his friend, Francis Oakley, a university student, spread the cause. Rogers gave up his curacy in order to give himself completely to the work, preaching from a waggon on St Peter's green, or a windmill on the Kimbolton road, till Mrs Oakley made available a barn behind her premises. She was a High Street milliner, a widow who had brought up five children by working hard at her business, and to her is attributed in Bedford the introduction of fixed prices instead of bargaining. At first new members had to go to London to be received. In 1745 the Bedford Moravian church was constituted, and soon afterwards a settlement, with a church, was built on the edge of the town, in what is now St Peter's Street, where members might fully carry into practice their idea of a Christian life. There were houses for single brothers and single sisters; there was daily worship; and all worked at trades to support themselves; while the children were taught. Church decisions were taken by lot.

Hardly had the Moravian settlement been established, when there came a new impetus in the form of what we now know as Methodism. William Parker, a grocer, who had at first been attracted by the Moravians, but was not able to go all the way with them, invited an Anglican travelling preacher whose reputation was growing, John Wesley, in 1753. Wesley preached both at Parker's house and on St Peter's green. He returned the next year. In 1758, soon after Parker's mayoralty, he preached the Assize sermon in St Paul's church. A group began to meet regularly in Parker's house, and Wesley to return at intervals, till in 1784 he found his old friend Parker 'quivering on the verge of life'. In this year the first Methodist national conference was held; and from this date, when Wesley ordained men for overseas work, began the separation of the Methodist societies from the Anglican church, becoming complete in 1795.

THE GAOL

This century had shown, by the events which led up to the formation of the Harpur Trust, that nonconformists could influence local affairs, although technically debarred from office. Bedford was also to show that the life of a single nonconformist could have national consequences: John Howard and prisons.[8]

As the county town, Bedford contained the county gaol, which was still the old building at the corner of Gaol Lane (Silver Street) and High Street. In 1751 the justices had some alterations made. Howard says there was a day room for debtors (who were confined here till they could pay their debts); and separate day rooms for men and women, without fireplaces. Down eleven steps were two dungeons, often damp. The prisoners slept on straw. No food was provided, but those who were entirely without resources could petition for the county bread. There were periodic outbreaks of gaol fever (typhus), and in the hope of combating this a ventilator was installed in 1754. Normally felons (as distinct from debtors) did not remain long in gaol; the death penalty, imposed for many offences, was usually commuted to transportation to the American colonies.

The gaoler (an annual appointment) had no salary, and even prisoners found innocent must pay his fees before they could be released. John Richardson, innkeeper of the *Chequers*, north of the gaol, was appointed 1711; and his sons John and Thomas frequently held the office till 1769.

In 1773 John Howard in his capacity of a modest landowner at Cardington was nominated sheriff. The holder of this office should by law take the Anglican sacrament, though since 1727 parliament had annually passed an act of indemnity for office-holders who did not. Howard accepted the office without taking the sacrament. He was surprised to find, as he sat in court during assizes, that innocent prisoners were led back to gaol till they could pay the gaoler's fees. There were in the gaol 8 debtors and 5 felons. To him it was obvious that the justices should pay the gaoler a salary, but their reply was that they had no precedent for authorising a salary. Hence he set off on tours of enquiry all over the country, and in 1774 parliament authorised gaolers' salaries and set free prisoners detained for non-payment of fees. Howard, his interest having once been fired, continued his widespread enquiries, and in 1777 produced a massive survey, the *State of the Prisons*. Extending his enquiries to Europe, he finally died at Kherson in Russia in 1790. His was the first statue erected in St Paul's cathedral.

At Bedford a salary of £60 per annum for the county gaoler

F

was introduced in 1785. Elsewhere movements for better prison buildings were on the way, but difficulties in Bedford held up plans for some years.

Besides the county gaol there was still the county bridewell or house of correction, where in theory vagabonds were set to work. This was in Caldwell Street. Here in 1745 Lucy Axtil, an incorrigible rogue, was sentenced to hard labour for six months, and to be whipped publicly every eight weeks (whipping was usually done from the pillory to the bridge).

The borough still had its own gaol, though no longer on the bridge. This gaol, the former chapel, was taken down in 1765; and another built in St Loyes.

THE TOWN IN GENERAL

By this century plague had died out. The main health hazard was smallpox, and there was a bad epidemic in 1738–9, when Francis Hunt, vicar of St Paul's, died. 'A great many now die', wrote the diarist, Rogers. He gives details also of a murder in 1730: 'Branklin, a pipemaker, was poisoned by his wife, who put arsenic into his hasty pudding . . . she run away as soon as she had done it'. There were traffic accidents; an apprentice riding too fast, rode down little Mary Hull, while a similar accident befell 6-year-old John Speechley from a butcher on horseback; both children suffered fractured thighs.

On a happier note, a number of clergy and gentry from a wide area round Bedford combined in 1703 to set up a library:[9] In all there were 62 trustees, and among those from the town were William Beckett, William Faldo, draper, and Thomas Battison. The list of books ran to about 300 items; mainly theology, but also classics, travel and biography; and in date they ranged from 1484 (Caxton) to 1703. They were to be kept in the vestry of St John's church, and to be lent out, two at a time, against a deposit, on Saturdays between 10 am and 4 pm, the rector of St John (Edward Bourne) acting as librarian. The books were soon transferred to a leasehold building in St Paul's Square, and when this lease ran out, were moved to St Paul's church. But, as so often happens with splendid schemes, enthusiasm waned; arrangements for renewal of the trust were neglected; and from 1780 to 1800 there were only four regular borrowers.

Horse-races were held in 1730 on Cow Meadow, 'there not having been one at Bedford before in anyone's memory'.

Sometimes accounts survive of merrymaking, at least for the well-to-do. Thus at a Bedford assembly in 1757 there were fourteen dances, including minuets, and the ball was opened by Lord Russell and Lady Caroline Russell. Numbers present on such occasions seem to have been few: in 1777 there were fifteen couples, though no doubt their elders were present in the cardroom. The refreshments included cake and coffee or tea; and at 10.30 pm there was a genteel cold collation. This ball ended at 3 am. It is not recorded where these gatherings were held – it may have been at the Sessions House, which was sometimes used for social occasions (the accounts mention clearing up after players).

There were in this century two modest charities to provide education for poorer children. The will of Alexander Leith (vicar of St Paul's), 1727, left money to educate 20 children, while Alderman Newton's bequest in 1760 was for 25. The latter soon ran into difficulties.

Another 18th century innovation was that, by the Militia Act of 1757, the names of local men were drawn by lot (in the town as in the villages). Those so selected underwent military training to enable them to undertake home defence in wartime in case of need. It was not till the Napoleonic wars that the militia was actually embodied for this purpose.

Of Bedford inns, that sometimes peevish diarist, John Byng describes them as 'cheap, civil and wretched', but he does say of his room at the *Swan* looking over the river that nothing could be more agreeable than 'the smoothness of the wide water, the skipping of the fish, and the sight of a party of elegant female rowers'.[10]

One 18th century Bedford character known to many (from the prominence of her gravestone in St Paul's churchyard – by the south porch) is Patience Johnson. She died in 1717 and was the wife of Shadrach Johnson who died in 1741. By his first wife he had 12 sons and 12 daughters, and by Patience 8 further children, making 32 in all. The *Arts Gazette* for 30 November 1741 records that he kept the *Wheatsheaf* inn and was said to brew the best beer in Bedford.[11]

A Bedfordian of whom one would like to know more is Samuel Bull who died in 1726. He possessed a Cremona violin, which he left – together with his flutes and oboe – to his friend Dr W. M. Turner of London, a musician and composer of national repute.

8 NOTES

Hist. Beds., 322–8.
1. *Lock Gate, loc. cit.*
2. C.R.O., WL.
3. C.R.O., OR 1883.
4. C.R.O., GA 2818 and BD 1073. Miss Anne Buck kindly drew my attention to this.
5. *B.H.R.S.*, xxx, 30.
6. G. Scott Thomson, *The Russells in Bloomsbury*, 208–33, shows Butcher's importance in London, but does not deal with his local influence.
7. See my *Harpur Trust.*
8. See my *John Howard*; also *B.H.R.S.*, lvi.
9. C.R.O., P 1/28/3; see also A. E. Baker, *Bedford Public Library and its forerunners.*
10. *Torrington Diaries*, iii, 201.
11. Cited *Beds. Archit & Archaeol. Soc.*, 1864, op. 208.

9   A Time of Change, 1790–1830

The period 1790–1830 saw marked changes. A break was made with the past, and at the same time expansion made easier, by enclosing the open fields which still surrounded the town. With a good communication system, trade expanded, and a bank was set up. An able headmaster came to the grammar school. The cumbersome system of civil parishes was amended, while a new body took over the planning of improvements for the town. As county town, Bedford was the site not only of a rebuilt gaol but of an infirmary or hospital and an asylum.

Change is accelerated by war – this was the period of the Napoleonic wars – and also is promoted by able and alert people. Bedford was fortunate at this time. One of the borough MPs was Samuel Whitbread junior; he succeeded his father in 1790 and continued to represent Bedford till his death in 1815. Not only was he able and well-to-do (the London brewery founded by his father giving him a secure financial basis, as well as his growing Bedfordshire estate), but he was concerned to use his advantages to serve the people of his county and county town, especially the more unfortunate. He was ably seconded by Theed Pearse, clerk both of the town council and of county quarter sessions. The name Pearse was to be notable for a century, as he was succeeded successively by son and grandson. He saw to the smooth running of affairs. Additional steam for some of Whitbread's projects was generated by the radical nonconformist writer, William Belsham, grandson of Thomas Woodward, and for a time Woodward's successor in the St Paul's Square brewery, which however he relinquished in 1800 to William Long – another active Bedfordian, but more of a traditional businessman. A newcomer to Bedford, Joseph Barnard, who had established himself as coal merchant by 1773, was to proceed to banking.

At this period everyone was within walking distance of everyone else. The tradesman lived above or behind his shop; the attorney did business from his house; and both the vicar of St Paul's and the headmaster of the grammar school lived in St Paul's Square. Only a few people were building large, pleasant houses on the edge of the town, some of which still remain in Cardington Road, or St Mary's former rectory in Cauldwell Street. There was congestion in the centre of the town, St Paul's church being surrounded by Stonehouse Lane, Butcher Row, Church Alley, Fishmarket, and Vines Corner; while the river west of the bridge was lined with wharves and breweries; and to the east were the rebuilt *Swan* and (on the south bank) Duck Mill. But within a few hundred yards in any direction was open country.

ENCLOSURE

This agricultural land surrounding Bedford no longer provided opportunity for Bedford tradesmen to carry on part-time farming. For the most part it belonged to county landowners, who let it to tenant farmers. North of the river, the largest of these owners was the Earl of Ashburnham, whose property of more than 300 acres is commemorated in Ashburnham Road. In the east, Bushmead Avenue recalls that William Gery of Bushmead Priory had about 80 acres here. The only Bedfordians with sizeable holdings were Jeremy Fish Palmer with nearly 200 acres, and John Hawes with over 100 acres. South of the river, the Duke of Bedford had over 100 acres, and Samuel Whitbread nearly as much.

The built-up area was little larger than formerly, the population being now nearly 4,000 (3,948 at the 1801 census). This area was mainly bounded by St Peter's and St Cuthbert's churches north and east, St Leonard's farm on the south, and St Loyes on the west. Close up to these came the open fields: Conduit, Windmill, Bury, Oak, Hole, Muswell and Mother Fields. Even though the strip system of mediaeval days had been much modified, no owner's land was entirely contiguous.

In the county generally, enclosure of such open field land reached its peak about 1800, and thus it was appropriate that similar action should be taken for the outlying agricultural area of Bedford. So in 1797 the parishes north of the river were enclosed (St Paul, St Peter and St Cuthbert); while St Mary's followed suit in 1799. St John's parish had no agricultural land.

One Bedford farmer was notable: John Foster of Brickhill (commemorated in Fosterhill Road). In 1807 he wrote a pamphlet *Observations on the agriculture of north Bedfordshire*. This is mainly a discussion of different soils and of the best way to deal with them. He also makes some general observations, commending improvements such as a better breed of sheep, and more up-to-date implements, all largely due to the regular Woburn meetings and the Bedfordshire Agricultural Society (founded in 1801). (He himself had a fluted iron roller commended by another farmer-writer, Batchelor.) He also shows a concern for better housing for farmworkers, and praises Whitbread for the 'comfortable habitations' on his estate. But he deplores the tendency to larger farms, by which 'respectable families are deprived of employment'.

COMMUNICATIONS

Modernising of the main roads, from tolls taken at turnpike gates, was completed. The road to Kimbolton was turnpiked in 1795; that through Goldington to join the Great North Road in 1814, as also that to Newport Pagnell and that to Northampton. Stage coaches plied along these roads. A directory printed in 1785 states that a coach leaves the *Swan* for London on alternate days (fare 12s or 6s 6d according to whether one travelled inside or outside). In 1787 the Duke of Bedford acquired the old *Swan*, and rebuilt it as the dignified building we know today; incidentally, he transferred to it the fine 17th century staircase from Houghton House which he was dismantling at the time. By 1824 (the date of the next surviving directory) there were five coaches for London leaving the *Swan* or the *Red Lion*, while other coaches plied to Cambridge, Oxford, Kettering and Leeds.

For one of these coaches – that from Kettering to London – the accounts survive. One of the partners was a Bedford man, John Rawlins. His papers reflect the cost of repairs to harness, lamp and windows; an occasional breakdown due to a broken axle-tree; and an ominous occasion 'when the man was lost in the snow'. In the winter of 1815 some passengers who dined at the *Swan* complained of only having cold beef and nothing hot. Rising fares were also a problem: in 1811 when the fare to London was raised by 1s, 'Mr Brooks of Bedford will not go with us now'.

Up the river lighters laden with coal and other goods continued to come to Bedford wharves, though occasionally hampered by bad weather.[1] In 1796 ice blocked the river for three weeks, and there was a bad flood in 1823. But some adverse effects for Bedford arose from the opening of the Grand Junction canal, which soon had wharves at Newport Pagnell and Leighton Buzzard. To counteract this, a public meeting was called by the mayor in 1811, and it was proposed to link Bedford with the Grand Junction by a canal fourteen miles in length, passing through Wootton, Marston and Lidlington. The cost was expected to be £100,000, and many doubted whether the traffic would be enough to justify this. £20,000 was promised, but opposition in the county grew. In 1813 Theed Pearse wrote to Whitbread 'I am afraid we must not flatter ourselves with the hope of proceeding'.

TRADE AND BANKING

In spite of the apprehensions aroused by the Grand Junction canal, trade was flourishing. Brewing was still important, the chief brewer being William Long, who acquired the St Paul's Square brewery in 1800. From 1784 he had been in partnership with the Whittingstall brothers, and in 1803 he bought out the surviving brother, James. One method by which they increased their trade was by buying up public-houses; already they had secured public-houses in a number of villages, while in Bedford itself they had the *Sow and Pigs*, *Hearse and Horses*, *Shoulder of Mutton*, *Castle*, *Wrestlers*, *Ship*, *Black Horse*, and two *Red Lions*. Long continued this policy, adding to his Bedford list the *Saracen's Head*, *Nag's Head*, *New*, *Haycock*, and the *New Ship* inn. When he died in 1841 he owned in all 28 public-houses.

Similarly the coal trade prospered. The county treasurer was still a Bedford coal merchant, William Watkins, 1793–1803. Even the old Herne chapel ended its days in this connection, being leased by Joseph Barnard as a storehouse. It was not surprising that a coal merchant should be the first to set up a bank in Bedford. A successful merchant who accumulated funds would occasionally be approached for loans, and Joseph Barnard was already giving such accommodation when John Byng applied to him in 1793:

'Oh Sir, what you choose – £150 or more'. So in 1799 with two partners Barnard formally set up a bank at the south-east corner of St Paul's Square.[2] Its capital was £10,000, and it acted as a collecting agency for the London money and stock markets. But in 1811 a stock market collapse brought Barnard into serious difficulties. His friend and adviser in the Bank of England, himself threatened, sold some of Barnard's securities, and the latter lost over £15,000. However, Barnard's bank did not actually fail, as many local banks did, and he learnt from this occasion not to take risks. His banking facilities were a help to many Bedford ventures, such as those of the Improvement Commissioners (see below),and for forty years his bank issued its own notes.

A comparison of the Bedford directory for 1785 and that for 1823 shows an expected increase in the food trades (bakers 8–14, butchers, 11–15), with a decline in some crafts, such as weavers and parchment-makers. Watchmakers increased from two to five. At the later date there are cabinet-makers, and also six milliners.

THE SCHOOLS

It was in this period that at last Harpur's endowment began to have an increasing effect on the schools,[3] especially the grammar school.

The writing school, set up in 1764 to provide teaching in English for boys not likely to enter the professions had prospered under the first master, George Jackson, until he was overcome by age and infirmity and died in 1803. At one time he had seventy-four boys in the ground floor of the old schoolhouse, about half of whom learned reading, writing and accounts, the remainder reading only.

But at the grammar school on the floor above, where Latin and Greek were taught, things were different. Two successive masters and their respective ushers had made little effort. The second of these, John Hook, wrote in 1792 'the number of boys has not amounted to more than six or seven at a time, in general, for these twenty years or more', In his last years he was crippled with sciatica. He died in 1810.

Now on the Harpur Trust there was determination to get a better system going. The grammar school would be of no use to the sons of Bedford professional men without an able master. Such a master could attract boarders, who would enlarge the school, while their boarding fees would improve his income and encourage his efforts. A committee of three, G. D. Yeats, mayor (a physician), Theed Pearse, and Dr Philip Hunt (incumbent of St Peter's), went to see the Warden of New College. In 1811 Dr John Brereton was appointed, from Blundells School at Tiverton.

To provide boarding premises, the master's stable and coach-house were converted to dining-room and dormitory, and the first boarder was a son of Theed Pearse. By 1820 there were fifty boarders, mostly from neighbouring counties, some from as far away as Devon. At first they had a single bed each; later, beds were shared. They had to bring six towels, and were allowed three changes of linen weekly. The Doctor, though kind, was stern. Food was ample, and on Sundays he himself carved. The housekeeper in cold winters would sometimes warm the boys' beds with a warming pan.

Meanwhile the number of day boys also rose. Some were sons of prominent Bedfordians – Wing, Trapp, Hillyard. Others were sons of new residents, especially of ex-servicemen. The first father in this latter group was Captain G. B. Trollope in 1822, who had six sons. In the following years, no less than fourteen captains followed suit. By the 1830s the admissions register shows that parents were living in a developing residential sector – mainly on the west (The Crescent, Priory Terrace, Adelaide Square), but also east in Kimbolton Road and Goldington Road. They came to be known as squatters.

The writing school had after Jackson's death had an unsatisfactory period, but in 1831 here too a notable headmaster was appointed. This was John Moore from Christ's Hospital, who in the next thirty years was to build up his school to rival even the improved grammar school in importance.

Still further educational responsibilities began to be undertaken by the Harpur Trust in this period. The trust income was higher than it had ever been. Moreover, in the country generally there was a movement to make education much more widely available than hitherto. It was increasingly felt that not merely middle-class children, but those of poorer parents should be educated. The first moves towards this were generally in Sunday schools, which at this date meant schools where children received education on

Sundays because on weekdays they would be at work, and Sunday was the only day available. In Bedford the only regular schools for poorer children were the small charity schools founded in the 18th century by Leith and Newton, and that run by the Moravians for their own children. In other towns attempts were now being made, especially through the churches, to set up additional schools. But Bedford seemed to think that the Harpur Trust ought to cope with this as well as with what it was already doing.

Indeed, the trustees themselves thought so. In 1815 they built, adjoining the children's home, a school for 250 boys (girls were to come only when the boys had a half-holiday).

ORGANISATIONAL CHANGES

The modern enquirer might suppose that, in such a developing town, the council would play an increasing role. But that was not in accordance with the thought of the times. Neither in Bedford nor elsewhere, had anyone envisaged the far-reaching functions town councils were to exercise in the 20th century. Hence it is at other institutions we have to look to find rationalisation and new ideas.

THE HARPUR TRUST REVISED

A notable change had taken place in the Harpur Trust machinery when a new enabling act was secured in 1793. This was mainly achieved by Samuel Whitbread, helped in this instance by William Belsham, a vigorous and independent thinker. It had become clear that those trustees who were elected by the five parish vestries were ineffectual. Now their number was increased to 18, and they were elected at the Sessions House at a meeting presided over by the mayor. The electors were £10 householders or £15 lease-holders, and there was no religious qualification (thus William Belsham was able to be a trustee). It was a notable step nearer to democracy as we understand it today. By it, elections for an important Bedford institution were controlled by rules similar to those introduced nationally for parliamentary elections in 1832 and for municipal elections in 1835.

However, it is one thing to provide democratic procedures, and another to induce men to use them, and to do so responsibly. Time was to show that in quiet times the number of electors attending to vote was almost nil, but if welfare payments were threatened feeling could run very high.

Under the new act, the old welfare provisions were continued on a slightly larger scale, commensurate with the growing income from what was now a prosperous residential area in Holborn. Thus, for instance, the sum to be spent on apprenticeships was increased from £600 to £700, and the annual distribution of hall money was put at £500. A new element was introduced – – the provision of almshouses to supplement those Bedford already had (Hawes and Christie). There were to be twenty alms-houses for ten men and ten women, who should receive a weekly allowance. But in addition to these, when in 1802 a disastrous fire made a number of Bedford people homeless, the trustees built forty-six houses to help the situation – and these were later con-verted to additional almshouses.

THE CIVIL PARISH

Another rational step was taken the year after the new Harpur act was passed. In 1794 a private act of parliament set up the Incor-porated Guardians of the poor of Bedford.[4] By this, the five parishes (Sts Paul, Peter, John, Mary, Cuthbert) were to act together for the care of the poor and to set up a House of Industry or combined workhouse.

The House of Industry (architect John Wing) was opened in 1796 on open land off Kimbolton Road. It was four storeys high, and could hold 200 persons. It had workrooms for trades, and schoolrooms for children. There was enough land for the able-bodied to be employed in garden and farm. A committee of twelve, chosen from inhabitants rated at £10 per annum, managed it, and this committee was to meet every Tuesday from 8–12 o'clock.

The first surviving minutes (from 1817) show that there were usually nine or ten present at the committee, including such pro-minent Bedfordians as John Trapp, banker, G. P. Nash, brewer, and J. Green. Parish difficulties were not entirely eliminated, for in 1824 St Peter's parish had not paid its quota, and the church-wardens and overseers were warned that, if this was not paid forthwith, proceedings would be taken. Outdoor relief, usually from 2s to 5s weekly, was authorised to a number of persons, sometimes blind, or ill, or lying-in.

Many examinations are recorded of applicants who appeared before the committee. The reason that Francis Facey, a horse-keeper of St John's parish, was in trouble was that his master, William Jones with whom he boarded, had been distrained on for rent, and had left, so Facey had lost both job and lodging; and as his master had paid him irregularly, he had no funds in hand. Facey had originally come to Bedford from Abbotsley. Another applicant, however, James Phillips, an unemployed whitesmith, married with two children, had moved to St Paul's from St Cuthbert's. Women applicants were usually pregnant, and frequently during the Napoleonic wars the alleged father was doing military service; thus Lucy Pickett of St Mary's said the father of her child was William Phillips, a fifer in the Bedfordshire militia, now quartered at Yarmouth.

IMPROVEMENT COMMISSIONERS

In other boroughs besides Bedford, the idea arose that temporary machinery was the best way to bring about needed changes, and thus arose the system of obtaining a private act of parliament to set up improvement commissioners. Bedford's was in 1803. Some of the commissioners, though not all, were also on the town council.

They included a wide range of prominent men, with an urge to bring Bedford up to date. There was Theed Pearse; the banker, Joseph Barnard; the brewers William Long and Peregrine Nash; the architect John Wing; the physician G. D. Yeats; and the farmer, John Foster. The act empowered them to raise rates up to 8d in the £ in any one year; to borrow funds; to take down the old guildhall; and to build a new bridge. They had set themselves considerable tasks.

A passing regret springs to mind for the centre of old Bedford that was swept away when St Paul's Square was cleared – or partially cleared, for total clearance was not achieved. The medieval guildhall was taken down, and the town council arranged to meet at the Sessions House till such time as a new guildhall could be provided. Much of the other property was very small, and perhaps mean; eighty-two houses were listed for demolition.

The whole enterprise as first planned proved over-ambitious. New powers were obtained for rates (1s in the £) and borrowing (£5,000), but it was impossible to build a new guildhall, and even a new bridge seemed beyond attainment. Loans were raised. Samuel Whitbread, one of the borough MPs, lent £2,000; so did the Duke of Bedford; and 27 county gentry lent smaller sums. The architect, John Wing, planned the bridge, but the cost was great. Some lenders converted their loans into gifts. It began to be felt that the whole thing was a great burden. When at last in 1813 the bridge was opened, there was no ceremony and no bands played; simply Whitbread walked over the bridge and the commissioners met him. Tolls to pay off the debt continued to be levied till 1835.

COUNTY TOWN

As county town, Bedford was the site of three notable new buildings: gaol, asylum and infirmary.

In spite of Howard's work, a new gaol was not built till 1801. Plans had been begun in 1786 in Howard's lifetime, the idea then being to expand on the existing site at the corner of Silver Street and High Street, but it proved difficult to acquire the land. Conditions in the gaol got worse, especially as (since the American War of Independence) it was no longer possible to transport convicts to the colonies there. In 1799 there was a bad outbreak of typhus, when the sufferers were provided with broth, sago, and even wine, and rushlights were supplied so that someone could sit up with them at night. After the outbreak, the place was fumigated. Then a new site (the present site) was chosen, at that time on the edge of the town. John Wing was given the assignment, which was to include both gaol and house of correction (from Cauldwell Street). Special improvements were bath, chapel, and facilities for executions by means of a movable machine on the roof of the turnkey's lodge. The move was made in 1801, and the first execution took place a few weeks later (the old gallows at Gallows Corner was taken down in 1802). Typhus however still occurred, as in 1816 and 1825. A treadmill was installed in 1821 in the penitentiary. By this time transportation had been resumed – now to Botany Bay.

Two years later (1803) came the opening of an infirmary or

hospital. This Bedford owed to a generous bequest of £8,000 from its former MP, the elder Samuel Whitbread. Again the younger Whitbread, with a committee of supporters, carried out the project, and again the architect was John Wing. There were fifty beds, four nurses, matron and surgeon. For use during operations the latter was provided with three pairs of oilskin sleeves. About £50 per annum was spent on leeches for blood-letting. By 1811 there was a physician (Dr Yeats) and two surgeons, who attended on Saturdays from 11 to 12 o'clock for the admission of patients. Constant efforts were needed to raise funds to keep the hospital going. Many, both in town and county, paid annual subscriptions, (£2 per annum entitled the subscriber to recommend a patient). About 1829 a fancy dress ball in Bedford raised £50, and a bazaar where the Marchioness of Tavistock had a stall produced as much as £500.

An asylum provided under the act of 1808 by county justices was a new departure. Till now there had been practically no pro-vision for the mentally ill, except when occasionally an individual was sent to Bethlehem hospital in London. Through Whitbread's energy as chairman of the justices' committee for this purpose, Bedford's was the second asylum to be opened in the country, (Northampton in 1811 being the first). Once more the architect was Wing. In the Ampthill Road, it had accommodation for sixty patients, and the equipment included handcuffs and strait waistcoats. There were however workshops where patients could be occupied.

THE TOWN IN GENERAL

That so much development should take place in a period of which more than half was overshadowed by war is a reminder that in those days war was remote from the generality of life. Yet some Bedford men were no doubt serving in what had been the 14th Foot, but was in 1782 renamed as the Bedfordshire Regiment (in 1809 the 16th Foot was substituted). Others certainly were in the militia, which for much of the period was stationed at the coast as a defence. The Sessions House served as a drill hall when soldiers were in Bedford, with some damage resulting to the forms and tables there, and in 1804 a militia depot was built in Castle Lane (now part of the Cecil Higgins Gallery). Indeed, it was believed in

Bedford that soldiers deliberately married Bedford girls for the sake of the marriage portions from the Harpur Trust, and then deserted them, but since marriage portions were drawn by lot (forty in any one year), some ingenuity would have been needed to trace girls successful in the draw who had not already a Bedford suitor lined up. Robert Newland, later mayor, fought at Waterloo.[5]

Amusements continued at Bedford in wartime. At dances, the waltz was superseding the minuet: a letter-writer says of a ball at Bedford that 'the waltz appeared the rage of the night'. There was also the occasional play given by a travelling company at the Sessions House, or in the yard of the *George* inn; other sites for dramatic performances were St Loyes, or a barn in the yard of the *Hop Pole* in Cauldwell Street. In 1809 the plays were *The West Indians* and *The Agreeable Surprise*. Visitors were allowed to see a private museum or collection of curiosities kept by the painter, James Read, in the 1790s. And in 1812 there was a performance of the *Messiah* in St Paul's church; this one was not well attended, but a later one in 1825 in aid of the infirmary, when musicians from elsewhere gave 'gratuitous assistance' (violins, violincellos, double bass and drums) did better, tickets selling at 2s 6d up to 16s 6d.

Among Anglican clergy at this period a notable figure was Philip Hunt, rector of St Peter's.[6] In his younger days he had taken part with Lord Elgin in bringing to England the 'Elgin' marbles from the Parthenon. In Bedford he was a wise and active figure in such capacities as trustee of the Harpur Trust and visiting justice at the gaol. At the Old Meeting the minister was Samuel Hillyard, who was also active as secretary of the Bedfordshire Bible Society. In 1797 the main nonconformist churches joined in the Bedfordshire Union of Christians. There was for a time in Bedford co-operation between Anglican and dissenting Sunday schools, and once a year the pupils assembled at St Peter's green and processed up High Street to St Paul's, where a collection was taken for their expenses. The Methodists (now separate from the Anglican church) built a place of worship in Angel Street (now Harpur Street) in 1804, and the area of the Bedford circuit was gradually reduced to a manageable size, Luton splitting off in 1808 and Leighton Buzzard in 1812. An example of their active workers is William Cumberland, shoemaker. Born at Odell, he settled in Bedford on his marriage; and in 1796 became a local preacher, besides being an energetic class leader. A surviving letter of his about 1830 says 'We are getting on famously at Bedford . . . crowds flock to our prayer meetings'. During this period a small Jewish community had settled in Bedford, barely enough to constitute a synagogue. With an un-Christian attitude, some townspeople objected to a Jewish girl applying to draw for a marriage portion. The legal question was referred to the Chancellor, who in 1819 ruled against such participation.

Parliamentary elections during this period were rowdy affairs. The formation of informed opinion was difficult in the almost total absence of media. (Some well-to-do townsmen probably took the *Gentleman's Magazine*, but most of those who took a paper would rely almost entirely on the *Northampton Mercury*, Bedford having no paper of its own). One reason for election violence is probably the combative instinct, all too often shown today at football matches. The other is that at an election beer flowed freely; even with an enlightened and concerned politician like Samuel Whitbread, his expenses at the *Swan* inn in 1802 came to £240, and included 500 bottles of port, 130 gallons of beer, and much broken glass. In the campaigns leading up to the Reform Bill of 1832 – so long delayed – feeling reached fever height. The recordership of Bedford (since Sir Robert Barnard's death) had again gone to a Duke of Bedford. One of his sons, Lord William, had for some years held one of the borough seats, but had been so slack in his duties and so careless of Bedford opinion that once more opposition to the house of Russell was in full swing. 'The people of Bedford will now teach the house of Russell that they can and will be free' – and this was in spite of the fact that the candidate now was not the ineffective Lord William but the concerned and responsible Lord John. Lord John was once even pursued by drunken opponents from whom he was rescued by William White (father of Mark Rutherford). The future Mark Rutherford, in his cradle in the room above his father's shop, was actually moved for safety when on election night a stone came crashing through the window. Lord John lost the seat by one vote (490), the successful candidates being W. H. Whitbread (515) and F. Polhill of Howbury (491). The Reform Act still left Bedford with the disproportionately large representation of two members, but put an end to the creation of freemen for political purposes (non-residents could vote only if they lived within seven miles); while the borough franchise was fixed at householders rated at £10.

A contrasting picture of life in Bedford is given by the diary of Catherine Young, who had come to live in Bedford in 1831 to educate her son Willy, aged 10. 'I took poor Willy to Dr Brereton to commence school as boarder'. She took a house on St Peter's green, and made friends with another school mother, Mrs Ommany. She played the harp, went to church where Dr Hunt preached, sometimes hired a pony or a boat, made excursions in the county as to the newly-made Swiss garden at Old Warden, and visited the poor.

9 NOTES

Hist. Beds., 441–6.
1. *Lock Gate, loc. cit.*
2. L. Pressnell in *Westminster Bank Review.*
3. See my *Harpur Trust.*
4. C.R.O., PUBZ 1–3.
5. J. Hamson, *Bedford Town & Townsmen*, 8.
6. *B. Mag.*, xv, 31.

10 The Railway Age, 1830–70

During this period Bedford more than doubled in population (1831: 6,959; 1871: 16,850). It was the railway age. Industry began. The health risks incidental to large towns became apparent. More schools were needed, and the Harpur endowment ran into difficulties. There were new public buildings. The franchise was further extended, and a growing and more educated electorate began to read newspapers and form clubs.

To meet the needs of growing numbers, speculative builders put up many small houses in narrow streets on the outskirts of the old town area. To 20th century eyes, these seemed mean, and recent clearance has swept many of them away to allow for high-rise flats, such as Beckett Court and for a new shopping centre, and for the present County Hall. The vicar of St Paul's, James Donne, in 1834 said that 'much land near the town had been sold in small lots for speculators who pay no attention to the comfort of occupiers, only to profit. There are rows of double cottages back to back'. Poor though these houses were, they were probably better than some formerly in the centre of the town and cleared in the early 19th century by the improvement commissioners. There was however serious overcrowding.

At the same time, some pleasant housing was being erected for well-to-do tradesmen or for incoming school-parents. Some of this still survives in The Crescent, Adelaide Square, The Grove, Goldington Road and Kimbolton Road. The town clerk, Theed Pearse junior, lived in Rye Close on the way to Kempston. John Howard the industrialist (see below), who in the 1837 directory is shown as living over his shop in High Street, with foundry behind, moved out to Cauldwell House. In Mark Rutherford's *Catherine Furze*, he describes Mrs Furze urging her husband to turn the parlour behind the shop into a countinghouse, and move to the outskirts. Thomas Barnard the banker went to Cople House.

It was in 1846 that the first railway came to Bedford. This was not Bedfordians' first chance to travel by railway, for the London–Birmingham railway in 1838 passed close to Leighton Buzzard, and a coach ran daily to Leighton to take would-be train passengers from Bedford. Railways so caught public imagination that all sorts of plans were afoot. In 1836 there was a proposal for a line from London to Boston via Bedford, and also one from Cambridge to Birmingham. George Stephenson came to Bedford in 1844. But branch lines and cross-country lines did not attract much national support. Bedford would have to take an initiative. So in 1845 a group of business men, including Robert Newland, the brewer, T. A. and T. J. Green, coal merchants, Thomas Barnard, the banker, Isaac Elger, George Witt and Henry Littledale, formed the Bedford Railway Company, and negotiated an agreement with the London & Birmingham company. If they could get a line to Bletchley built, the bigger company would take it over. The first turf was ceremonially cut midway at Husborne Crawley. There was difficulty at the Brogborough cutting, but the line was opened in 1846 on 17 November. Church bells rang, Bedford Brass Band played, and large crowds watched 600 people in 30 carriages drawn by two engines leave for Bletchley. The passengers inspected the building of Bletchley station, then in progress, and returned to Bedford, where the Duchess of Bedford received them, and the great day concluded with a dinner. The journey from Bedford to Euston now took $2\frac{1}{2}$ hours.

Direct communication with London still had to wait some years. At first there was another indirect route through Sandy, through which the Great Northern line ran from 1850, and one could get an omnibus from Bedford to Sandy. Then in 1857 the Midland line from Leicester to Hitchin was opened, making contact there with the Great Northern line to London. Again there was a ceremonial journey, and the passengers were hospitably entertained at Leicester. At last in 1867 a Midland goods line via Luton to St Pancras came into operation, and the passenger service followed in 1868.

Meanwhile the Bedford–Cambridge line was opened in 1862. Last of all came the line from Bedford to Northampton. Here

Northampton took the initiative, the mayor of Northampton presiding over a meeting at Olney in 1864, and the line was opened in 1872.

Proposals which had fallen by the way included railways to Ely, Biggleswade, Wolverton and others – so vast was the network imagined. But there were many pitfalls on the way. An act had to be passed. Plans must be prepared and deposited for public inspection with the clerk of the peace (those of one abortive railway were deposited at 11.46 pm 30 November 1845 – the deadline being midnight). Money had to be raised. It is likely that many well-to-do Bedfordians invested in railway stock, but in that of the more important lines.

The construction of railways was beset with accidents to the navvies working on them, and in 1855 the Bedford infirmary applied to the contractors of the Bedford–Leicester line for an annual subscription, because of the very severe accidents they had had to cope with. When operational, railway travel was not as smooth or safe as today. Charles Dickens in 1867 got out of the train at Bedford because of 'the violent rocking of the carriages' – the Bedfordian, James Howard, retorted that the Bedford line 'runs as smoothly as any I have ever journeyed by'. One early accident was in 1862, when an excursion train returning from Bedford regatta ran into some cattle trucks.

As the railways developed, the roads declined. On the Saturday after the opening of the Bedford–Bletchley line in 1846, the *Bedford Times* coach, with its rose pink upholstery and green curtains, left the *Swan* inn for London for the last time. Its speed was 10 miles an hour, but now the public could catch trains at 20 miles an hour. In 1846 there were ten coaches running through Bedford. The 1854 directory lists only carriers to the villages and omnibuses and flies meeting trains.

Firms making carriages still had work for private traffic on local roads, and carts were needed for farmers. The 1854 and 1869 directories show the coach builder, Charles Deane, in St Mary's Square.

The turnpike trusts ran into difficulties: tolls could not pay for the upkeep of the roads. But clearly the main roads could not be suffered to become completely derelict. So in 1862 the government empowered quarter sessions to set up a system of highway boards. In Bedfordshire five such boards were set up, of which one was for Bedford and the surrounding parishes. The highway boards were not at all popular, and Bedford Highway Board in 1877 sent in to quarter sessions a resolution that, in their opinion, the system was an expensive failure, and it would be better to go back to the days of parish surveyors.

River navigation declined also.[1] It had already been affected by the Grand Junction Canal, which had by 1840 caused some Bedford merchants to set up wharves at Newport Pagnell. Now coal and other heavy goods went by railway. There were not enough tolls to keep the locks in repair. At first the proprietors could not even sell their rights – no one was interested. But in 1867 a purchaser was found who offered £1,500.

GAS AND INDUSTRY

Gas came to Bedford in 1832. Active businessmen wanted to introduce this new source of energy to the town, and formed a Bedford Gas Company. Shares were £30 each, and the capital was £6,000. Among the shareholders were not only John Howard the ironmonger and foundry owner, but also attorneys, like Alexander Sharman, and the surgeon Isaac Hurst. Gasworks were set up on the edge of the then town in what is now Greyfriars. The streets were lit with gas lamps. At first there was nervousness among private subscribers from possible danger from gas in the home, but by 1841 private consumption was nearing £1,700 per annum. New and enlarged works became necessary, and in 1864 the undertaking was transferred to Ford End Road. The Gas Company, like other customers, transferred their custom from water to railway. At first their coal came up the river, but in 1859 they signed a contract with the Midland Railway.[2]

The first considerable industrial venture came with John Howard and his sons, and the establishment of the Britannia Works. These Howards were a Bedford family (not related to the prison reformer, who came from Hackney), and John Howard's father had been gaoler of the county gaol. The boy, John, in 1805 was successful in drawing a Harpur Trust lot for apprenticeship, and was apprenticed to an Olney ironmonger. In 1813 he set up in business in Bedford on the west of High Street, and in 1817 moved across the street to a bigger site where he could put up a small foundry. Here he began to produce small goods, such as stoves and railings; and from them proceeded to farm implements.

His great success came with a new plough. This period was a thriving one for agriculture, with great landlords interested in farming improvements, and before the age of large-scale importation of corn from Canada. The actual plough design for which Howard became famous was first executed by a Wilstead blacksmith for the farming family of Armstrong. Howard saw its possibilities, and was able to produce and market it on a large scale. Shown at the Royal Agricultural Society's show in 1839, it became known as the champion plough of England. When the Britannia Ironworks were opened on the way to Kempston in 1859, it began to command an export market also, and further farming improvements of many kinds followed. When Garibaldi, hero of the Italian Risorgimento, came to Bedford during James Howard's mayoralty, 1863-4, it was to see steam-ploughing demonstrated by Howard's steam-engine. He planted a sequoia at the Britannia Works. In 1866 the firm won first prize at an International Steam Ploughing match near Lyons.[3] An article in the *Illustrated London News* in 1874 describes the works site as occupying 15 acres, where thousands of tons of iron were worked up into implements suited to different soils and climates.

There was also a smaller works, the Victoria Works, in Mill Street, built by E. Page.

The coal trade continued to be important. It was still a coal merchant (Francis Green, 1803-36, T. A. Green, 1838-41) who acted as county treasurer. Important also was brewing. Sir William Long died in 1841, and his brewery eventually went to T. Jarvis. Other brewers appearing in the directories of 1854 and 1869 are George Higgins on Castle Hill, Newland in St Paul's Square, and Nash in St Mary's.

Barnard's bank prospered, and a new Bank Building for it was opened at the foot of the bridge. Humbler folk were encouraged to save. In 1860 a Penny Bank was established, open two evenings a week, where savings could be made in pennies.[4]

PROBLEMS OF GROWTH

Growth poses problems – of employment, of health, of safety, and of education. Though the government's municipal corpora-

119

tions act of 1835 revised the town's machinery (councillors were henceforward elected for three years by ratepayers, aldermen for six years by the council, and the mayor annually by the council), additional powers had not been conferred – save that a borough police force was set up. In 1835 the rate income (a precept on the poor rate) was under £500, with another £500 from rents and tolls, and the town clerk was paid £50. The improvement commissioners were still in being, and not merged with the council till 1860. How then were these various problems dealt with?

UNEMPLOYMENT AND POVERTY

Unemployment does not seem to have been as serious a factor in Bedford as it was in the surrounding villages, where at the beginning of this period distress and even violence were rampant. (One reason for increase of population in both town and country was that the danger of smallpox had been largely overcome by the introduction of vaccination – free from 1840; and so more children lived to grow up). From an over-populated countryside, villagers came flooding into Bedford. Since there were not in the town outbreaks of violence comparable to those in the villages, it might be said that Bedford absorbed both its own natural increase and these arrivals. As has been seen, there were growing opportunities for employment in Bedford. But it is probable that many nominally employed lived on the verge of subsistence, or as we should now say, below the poverty line. For these, the Harpur Trust annual distribution of hall money, the provision of sixty-six almshouses, and even the payments obtainable for apprenticeship and for marriage portions, were of vital importance – hence the passions aroused in Bedford when the Harpur Trust ran into difficulties (see below). Moreover, these poorer families were losing the subsidiary income girls had earned by lacemaking at home, for machine lace could now be manufactured more cheaply than they could make it. Evidence given before the reform of the poor law in 1834 states that 'the only manufacture in Bedford is lace-making . . . very much declined of late . . . Formerly a very good worker could earn from 3s to 5s a day, now with difficulty 2s 6d a week'.[5]

When the poor law was reformed, Bedford was involved with the villages. The act of 1834 associated, for poor law purposes, nearly all north Bedfordshire with the town in the Bedford Union.[6] In other unions, such as Ampthill or Biggleswade, it was necessary to build a large Victorian workhouse, but the House of Industry, built under the act of 1793 in Bedford, was so extensive that, with a very little alteration, it served for the new Union. In fact, the contractor was desired in October to complete necessary alterations by December. Village workhouses were sold. Two relieving officers were appointed, one for the northern part of the union area, and one for the south, and Bedford came under the latter.

At first the guardians met at the House of Industry, but they found it too far to walk up the Kimbolton Road after stabling their horses in Bedford, so they changed the venue to the Sessions House. The vice-chairman was Isaac Elger of St Mary's (the chairman being a county man). They were soon in touch with an agent in Manchester, to help unemployed to transfer to the manufacturing districts of the north. Further plans followed to assist emigration overseas. All this mainly applied to the villages of the Bedford Union, but we do find in correspondence references to individual Bedfordians emigrating: thus in 1846 James Partridge went to Australia from Bedford St Paul's; and in 1851 from St Mary's the Thomas family, parents and five children, all under 14 years of age. Assisted emigrants received help with their passage; also a knife, fork, spoon and plate for the voyage, which (if they behaved well) they were allowed to keep. But, though there was some emigration, assisted or private, still Bedford's population more than doubled in 40 years.

There was a residue, consisting of the old, infirm, and children (for whom teaching was provided) in the House of Industry – usually fewer than 200. A newspaper account of Christmas Day 1859 says the hall was decorated, and the meal consisted of beef and plum pudding. After grace, the mayor, John Howard, and Alderman Hurst made long speeches, after which an inmate made a short speech of thanks. The children had oranges and nuts.

From the middle of the century, one factor improved for poorer families – a partial come-back of the pillow lace craft which had provided subsidiary income. Simpler and coarser lace, quicker to produce and resembling that of Malta, began to be made locally, though even with this long hours of work were needed for meagre payment. The firm of Charles and Thomas Lester at 115 High Street for many years provided a centre for the collection and disposal of this lace.

HEALTH AND SAFETY

In the town, as opposed to the surrounding villages, a greater problem than unemployment was that of health, when an increasing number of people were crowded together. The problems of hygiene and sanitation were not yet understood, nor was the importance of pure water. Houses still depended on private or public wells for their water supply. Slops were often thrown out of the door. Except for the larger houses, sanitation was by earth closets. Mark Rutherford says there was one sewer down High Street, which was discharged into the river at the foot of the bridge, where filth accumulated.[7] Graveyards were overcrowded. The result of all this was that, if cholera appeared, it spread rapidly. When there was an outbreak in 1832, the mayor circulated health hints: these included cleanliness, sleeping with closed windows, avoiding salads, and wearing flannel. In a worse epidemic in 1849, the death rate in St Paul's parish quadrupled, especially in small streets like All Hallows lane, Gravel lane, Newnham, Hawes and Thames Streets. When the cholera abated, public thanksgiving was made on 15 November.[8]

The provision of a piped water supply might – it was at first thought – be arranged by a company like the Bedford Gas Company. An attempt to form a company was made in 1859, and plans for waterworks were prepared. Such however was the ignorance of the time that there was a storm of protest at such mad extravagance (as indeed there was in the same period in Luton and other big towns at similar proposals, though Leicester had introduced piped water). Then came an outbreak of typhoid, so severe that the Privy Council called for a special report. The report showed that there were in the town 3,000 cesspools, and that wells inevitably were often near them. Even *The Times* of London made comments on the situation in Bedford.

The town council was now becoming alive to the health functions it could perform. Government action encouraged it, in so far as either local health boards could be set up, or an existing town council could obtain the powers of a health board. So Bedford town council did this in 1862.

That proper steps were taken over water was mainly due to the Howards of Britannia Works – John Howard being mayor at the time. His son James carried a proposal to send a deputation to Leicester to make enquiries into the system there. The reforming party on the town council took over the plans originally prepared for the proposed water company, and in 1866 waterworks were established on the Clapham road, while main drainage was put in hand.

About the same time the problem of congested graveyards was dealt with.[9] It was said in 1852 that in St Mary's not thirty spaces were left, and that in fact the graveyard had been re-used time and again. This time a burial board was set up, and in 1853 a site was chosen on Foster's hill, and a loan of £4,000 was obtained from Barnard's bank. The cemetery was opened 5 June 1855, all existing graveyards in the town being closed by order of the Privy Council.

Fire risk, though greatly increased by the size of the town, was not considered a municipal responsibility. The risk however was now more than a parish could cope with, so volunteer action was taken. Bedford Volunteer Fire Brigade was formed in 1869.

The infirmary or hospital also still relied on voluntary support. For treatment there it was necessary to get a letter of recommendation from a subscriber who paid a guinea a year, or to be recommended by a benefit club. (Benefit clubs were often associated with churches, for instance there was one at Howard Congregational Church). When in 1854 it was proposed to spend £30 on a new facility, a microscope, it was found that funds did not suffice. However it was found possible in 1848 to open a fever hospital.

Minor ailments were often treated at the Provident Dispensary, where medical advice was given to members (with wages below 25s weekly), who paid a penny a week for one person, or 3d for the family.

EDUCATION

Education for all children was beginning to be seen as a vital need in a society yearly becoming more sophisticated.[10] This in itself was a great challenge, but it was made far more serious by the fact that Bedford's population more than doubled in forty years. There were two further complicating factors. Bedford had become accustomed to leave all educational matters to the Harpur Trust. Whereas in other towns of comparable size, groups (mainly religious) were getting together to raise money to set up schools, practically no such voluntary attempt was made in Bedford. It seems that benefactions can have an enervating effect on the recipient. The other complicating factor was that, while far more money was now needed for general education, the Trust's income had become more or less stationary. The last act of parliament to revise the Trust's scheme was in 1826, and the scheme then authorised simply envisaged that income would continue to rise and that expenditure would continue on existing lines. In fact, income was stationary, while there was far greater need for expenditure. The trustees were caught in a situation they had not foreseen.

The period began well, with a splendid new complex of premises in what we now call Harpur Street. They were designed by Edward Blore, the first part being opened in 1833. Here were an office for the Trust's clerk, premises for the commercial (former writing) school, for the elementary school set up in 1815, and for the children's home.

At the elementary school the boys were at first taught by Furze, the master of the children's home, and from 1824 he had an assistant. In 1831, with the help of 19 monitors, they were teaching 289 boys. (Monitorial teaching was largely mechanical, the monitors passing on to the boys what they had learned from the masters, but its cost was minimal). Then Furze retired, and was replaced by Riley, who came from a national school at Westminster, and stayed till 1869. Riley said afterwards that he found many children ignorant of their letters or of simple arithmetic. Under him, soon many were able to write; he expanded the curriculum, got maps, and borrowed books. By 1869 he was teaching French and drawing.

Meanwhile, after a long struggle by reformers among the trustees, a girls' school was opened in 1836 with 265 girls, and a wing built for it in Well Street (Midland Road) in 1840. Here the headmistress 1836–60 was Mrs Furze. The occasional teaching given to some girls from 1815 – mainly needlework – was now expanded to full-time instruction in reading, writing and arithmetic; and in the 1860s, when Mrs Furze had been replaced by Miss Mitchell, and numbers were over 400, history and geography were also taught. A local inspector, the Rev. Fitzpatrick, gave it the highest praise.

An infants' school, which opened with 264 children, functioned on the ground floor of the new wing, until growing numbers at the girls' school forced them out of this section into temporary premises elsewhere.

In 1868 the numbers taught in the Trust's three elementary schools were:

boys	370
girls	490
infants	250
	1,110

At the boys' school there were three teachers. Thus much was done in this period by the Harpur Trust for elementary education.

The commercial school also developed greatly under John Moore, and it was necessary in 1860 to put up a new building for its junior section of over 200 boys – this was behind the main Harpur complex. There was to some extent an educational ladder: some boys went on from the elementary school to the commercial school. In 1850, out of 91 leavers, 55 went to work, 3 were apprenticed, 14 went to the commercial school, 2 died of cholera, and several left the town. Only for girls was there no provision beyond the elementary stage, except what could be had by paying fees at the Moravian school or at a private school.

But a financial crisis came in the 1840s. Since in London the fashionable residential area had moved west of Holborn, while commercial possibilities had not yet developed there, income was stationary. Welfare payments were fixed under the 1826 act as: hall money £500; apprenticeship £1,500; marriage portions £800; besides which were the sixty-six almshouses and the children's home. In fact, the marriage portions were an anachronism, and the apprenticeship system was declining. But, these amounts having legal sanction, there was no way to finance expansion in the education service. In 1843 the debt was £9,000. In 1848 Barnard's bank refused to make further advances.

What aggravated the situation was that, in an earlier period at the grammar school, to encourage the headmaster there he had been allowed a capitation fee of 5 guineas for each boy. Under the able master, Dr Brereton, numbers grew so much that the capitation fees added £1,000 to the Trust's obligations to him, and £800 to the usher's salary. In 1852/3 the grammar school cost over £3,000; the other schools £1,865; and welfare work £5,607.

There was no way out of the situation except by a new act or scheme, which would empower the Trust to cut its coat according to its cloth. Yet how was it possible to get agreement for this?

On one side were the professional men like Alexander Sharman, the substantial businessmen, and the squatters, backed by New College. On the other were small tradesmen: the draper, George Hurst; the hairdresser, John Mantel; the veterinary surgeon Charles Dines; and all the humbler folk in Bedford who benefitted from the Trust's welfare work. In 1848 a public meeting of 430 persons signed a memorial against sacrificing the welfare side 'to extend the education of the rich'.

At last in 1853 a new scheme was adopted by order of Chancery. It was an inevitable compromise. Some concession was made from the supporters of the grammar school in that capitation fees were not to be paid for boys above the number of 167. But the main change was on the welfare side: hall money ceased: and apprenticeship fees and marriage portions were reduced.

THE CHURCHES

Churches were enlarged and new churches built. St Paul's tower and spire were rebuilt in 1868. The little old church of St Cuthbert, too small to accommodate incoming numbers in the parish, was replaced in 1847. (A recent incumbent of St Cuthbert's, 1822–31, was Archdeacon Tatham, who, incidentally, on his retirement travelled in Egypt and Palestine, and collected manuscripts which he gave to the British Museum). To meet expansion on the west of Bedford, Holy Trinity was opened in 1841. In 1837 Anglican dioceses were revised, and Bedford was transferred to that of Ely.

For other denominations provision was expanded also. The Old (Bunyan) Meetinghouse was remembered by Mark Rutherford as crowded and uncomfortable in his boyhood – he also recalled the orchestra there, double bass, bassoon and flute, while the note was given with a tuning-fork. This church was rebuilt in its present dignified form in 1849, and was later presented by the Duke of Bedford with handsome bronze doors depicting scenes from *The Pilgrims Progress*. Here as minister came in 1864 John Brown, a grand figure, who, during his forty years' incumbency, was to write the life of John Bunyan, and also to continue collecting Bunyan editions and relics. He lived in the manse in Dame Alice Street. The New (Howard) Meeting was also enlarged in 1849. The rebuilding of the Methodist church in Harpur Street had come even earlier – 1831. A notable family here was that of the industrialists, Howard. John Howard continued as a local preacher in surrounding villages till old age. The Moravian church was extended in 1865. Among the dissenting churches there was some co-operation over Sunday School teaching: in 1860 all dissenting churches in Bedford were combined in a Sunday School Union.

Towards the end of the period Roman Catholicism re-established itself in Bedford. By 1863, Father J. P. Warmoll was living in a single room in Offa Street and saying mass for a congregation of about twenty in a washhouse near the prison. In 1865 a site in Brereton Road was bought for a church.

Besides the above there were several new developments. An unusual figure of the time was Timothy Matthews, originally an Anglican curate, who acquired such a following that his supporters built him a church in Bromham Road (now converted to lay purposes), to which he summoned worshippers by blowing a trumpet in the streets. There was a new Baptist chapel in Mill Street, one in Cauldwell Street, and a Particular Baptist one in Castle lane. A Primitive Methodist chapel was opened in Hassett Street in 1838, while 1837 saw a Catholic and Apostolic church. The small group of Jews who had come to Bedford at the end of the last century still managed intermittently to hold a synagogue as often as their numbers permitted.[11] (It is pleasant to note that from 1833 the Harpur Trust disregarded the former Lord Chancellor's ruling against Jews, and began again to admit Jewish children to the schools).

A national religious census taken in March 1851 gives some idea of the relative position of denominations.[12] The attendance at morning service on this particular Sunday was:

Anglicans	1,371
Congregationalists	1,095
Methodists	800
Baptists	512
Moravians	280
Catholic & Apostolic	80
Timothy Matthews	70
	4,208

The population was then 11,693. It may be doubted whether, in the much larger Bedford of today, there are 4,000 at worship on Sunday morning.

NEW BUILDING

A number of other new buildings arose besides churches. First were the stately Assembly Rooms in Harpur Street in 1834, now restored to their original purpose. In 1836 there was transferred to two rented rooms in this building the old library. This had had an uncertain period. Already in 1817 the discovery was made that the valuable manuscript cartulary of Newnham Priory had by unknown means arrived at the British Museum. At one time the library was housed over a butcher's shop in St Mary's; there was a librarian, John Mayle, at a salary of six guineas, and subscriptions were a guinea yearly. Then in 1831 the vicar of St Paul's got permission to transfer it. Now it entered on its last stage. In 1861 subscribers numbered less than one hundred, and it was amalgamated with a society of high-sounding name – Bedford Literary and Scientific Insitute.[13]

In 1848 came the rebuilding of the prison.[14] By 1841 the death sentence was abolished for almost every offence but murder; and transportation overseas was to cease in 1857. Thus the usual sentence was imprisonment with hard labour, and more accommodation was required. But the responsibility was still that of county justices, and they hesitated to incur the expense (as they did for a new Sessions House – there were already complaints of the old one). To the rebuilt prison there soon came a remarkable man as governor, R. E. Roberts, who in the course of his time there compiled criminal statistics for the century. Local responsibility for the prison was to cease in 1877.

Another county building which had become outgrown was the asylum. It had been so successful that Hertfordshire and Buckinghamshire had asked to share in it. In 1857 there were 307 patients. A bigger and more central site for the three counties was found at Arlesey, and to this the patients (now 422) were moved in 1860. The old site became the first building estate south of the river. At the end of the century (1899) the old infirmary was replaced by a new building.

In this period of high farming, Bedford as an agricultural centre felt the need of a Corn Exchange. A company was formed, and a small hall built on St Paul's Square in 1849. It was not in fact large enough for its purpose.

LIFE IN GENERAL

At the beginning of this period, a town crier was still in occasional use to give out notices for the town, and one postman sufficed to distribute Bedford's letters (the old post office was in the Fishmarket). Soon a need began to be felt for a local paper. The first was the *Bedford Mercury* in 1837. Then in 1845 came the *Bedfordshire Times*. Bedford still returned two members to parliament till 1885; one was usually liberal (frequently a Whitbread), and one conservative (Polhill or Stuart); ie, both came from county families. But in 1868, after the franchise had been extended in 1867, James Howard was one of the representatives, and Bedford Reform League celebrated his victory with a banquet. The hustings were on St Peter's Green, and until 1872 voting was still public. The rival parties processed up High Street wearing rosettes and carrying banners. Sometimes there was horseplay among the crowd, and in 1851 the liberal (later mayor) George Hurst was accidentally knocked down.

Festivals likewise were celebrated in public, and in 1863 when the Prince of Wales was married, over a thousand people sat down to dinner in High Street, and others in St Mary's and St John's.[15] Guns were fired, bells rang, and bands played. The Britannia Works entertained 1,500 children. However, a fiasco followed at night when fireworks were to be let off on St Peter's Green. These had been stored in a barn, and by some accident all went off at once; there was 'a great burst of flame, a terrific explosion, and the whole interior of the barn looked like a furnace of hissing fiery snakes'.

Bedford races were still held on Cow Meadow till about 1874. A race-stand was provided by a race-stand company, and there was also a refreshment room. Several race cards have survived. There began to be other forms of organised sport. At first the regatta was informal. We know there was one in 1848, because of an accident caused by a small boy running across the bridge to see the boats, with the result that a horse, pulled up too sharply, bolted. By 1853 the regatta was formal, but many boats leaked, and had to be baled out. In 1869 a girl who ran in front of the starting gun was accidentally killed. By this time, bicycles had come into use, and there were said to be an enormous number in Bedford. Sometimes town and county joined in new associations, as in the Town and County Cricket Club, 1870.

Music too claimed its associates. In 1836 Bedford Harmonic Society began to organise six concerts a year at the Assembly Rooms. This society seems to have declined, but in 1866 arose a new one, the Bedford Musical Society, president Frederick Howard; its conductor for many years was P. H. Diemer. And Bedford Brass Band was in evidence on all ceremonial occasions.

Topographical art owes much to Bradford Rudge, who in 1839 came to teach drawing at the commercial school, and later taught it also at the grammar school, besides taking private pupils.[16] His watercolours evoke the Bedford of the period.

Serious studies were fostered by the Workingmen's Institute, opened in Harpur Street in 1856, with a library of 2,000 volumes. Temperance claimed a large following. Bedford Band of Hope was founded in the 1850s. Each band had a banner, and its members wore a white brooch. Local Bands of Hope were formed into a union in 1872. A Building Society was set up to help the small house purchaser.

Yet much was rough in the life of the time. There was even in 1859 a running battle at St Peter's Green between the boys of the grammar and commercial schools over the shared use of a hired playing-field north of the town (the educational possibilities of sport were just beginning to be realised), and one boy was knocked unconscious. Public executions still took place outside the prison.

When in 1860 a Luton man was executed for the murder of his wife, an 'immense concourse' began to gather from early in the morning for the execution at noon. The Rev R. W. Fitzpatrick of Holy Trinity addressed the crowd. The last public execution was that of William Worsley in 1868.

Already some Bedfordians were looking to a wider world. Such was F. G. Burnaby, who in 1875 rode 300 miles in mid-winter across the steppes to Kabul and India, described in his *Ride to Khiva*.

10 NOTES

Hist. Beds., 484–98.
1. *Lock Gate*, ii, 20.
3. *Op. cit.*, ii, 16–18.
3. J. Hamson, *Bedford Town & Townsmen*, 102.
4. Hamson, *op. cit.*, 92.
5. Mr P. Grey kindly drew my attention to this.
6. For the following, see C.R.O., PUBM 1 and PUBC 2/5–6.
7. M. Rutherford, *Early Life*, 13.
8. Hamson, *op. cit.*, 72.
9. Hamson, *op. cit.*, 79.
10. See my *Harpur Trust*, and *B.H.R.S.*, liv.
11. *B. Mag.*, xv, 69.
12. *B.H.R.S.*, liv.
13. A. E. Baker, *Bedford Public Library and its forerunners.*
14. *B.H.R.S.*, lvi.
15. Hamson, *op. cit.*, 99.
16. *B. Mag.*, xvi, 101.

11   Anglo-Indian Bedford, 1870–1914

GROWTH

In this period Bedford again more than doubled (1871: 16,850; 1911: 39,183). Part of this growth was intake from the villages, but less than in the previous forty years, for the population of most villages was now either stationary or declining. Much was due to natural increase, since health conditions now offered better prospects of survival. Growing industry attracted some. And one major factor was the special position Bedford now assumed as an educational centre. For the first time, housing was seen as to some extent a public responsibility: early development was slow, but from 1890 boroughs could initiate housing schemes. Much building was still done by private developers however; for instance, in 1881 Joshua Hawkins bought land north of Bromham Road, which had formerly been closes, and the Lansdowne Road area developed – nos 1–30 are given in the 1892 directory. More amenities appeared.

COMMUNICATIONS

It was the peak period of railways, the network of which was now complete. The management of the main roads leading to Bedford was taken over in 1888 by the newly formed County Council and their upkeep began to be improved after the uneasy times of the highway boards. Farmers from the surrounding villages drove on Saturdays into Bedford, putting up pony and trap at an inn on the outskirts, such as the *Fountain* opposite St Mary's church. Other villagers walked or came by carrier; it was said at Dean that those who walked got home as soon as those who rode with the carrier, since the latter stopped at a public-house in every village. Bicycles multiplied. A few motor cars appeared. When driving licences were issued in 1904, the first Bedfordian to obtain one was a commercial traveller, Lawrence Taylor, and he was followed on the same day by the young S. R. Wells, later to be MP for

Bedford (1922–45).[1] Over 150 driving licences were issued in the year. On the river two pleasant little pleasure steamers plied – the *Lodore* and the *Lady Lena*.

INDUSTRY

Industry expanded. First came W. H. Allen's engineering works in 1894, with 13 acres near the railway. In 1907 W. H. A. Robertson, then working with a Birmingham firm, set up his own works in Bedford. The Igranic Electric Co came in 1913, succeeding Adam's Motors. In 1913 came also the Meltis factory. The concentration of brewing in fewer and larger firms continued: the Horne Lane brewery, which Jarvis secured in 1873, was in 1910 acquired by Charles Wells, while Newland took over Nash. In banking, a few large national banks were extending their empire, but the local bank of Barnard continued throughout this period to function in Bank Buildings.

A local activity which had passed its peak was the manufacture of agricultural implements. At the beginning of the period, this was not apparent. Indeed, when in 1874 the Royal Agricultural Society's show was held in Cow Meadow, the great time of farming seemed to have reached its apogee, and in the same year a new and larger Corn Exchange was opened in St Paul's Square (the previous small one, now known as the Floral Hall, was pulled down in 1904). But already large-scale importation of corn from Canada was beginning to send English farming into a depression, and the effect of this was increasingly felt in Bedford at the Britannia Works.

The town was still small enough to be a close-knit community. In the smaller shops, like Clarke the grocer in Harpur Street or Lansberry the shoe shop in St Mary's, there was a personal relationship between shopkeeper and customer. Even the bigger shops were kept by local families: the drapers, Braggins and Rose, the grocer Dudeney, and the bookshop kept by Hockliffe. Such shops can be found in the directories of 1885 and 1894 and later. There were still to be seen glimpses of an earlier Bedford: the stone archway of the former mediaeval *George* inn, the overhanging *White Horse* inn at the corner of Harpur Street and Midland Road, and the 17th-century shop front of Sell & Wilshaw's in High Street.

It was at this time that the government first laid down that a general education service was to be a public responsibility.[2] For the first thirty years, however, town councils were not involved. By an act of 1870 elected school boards were to be set up wherever (and this was almost everywhere) there was not adequate provision. At the same time the government enquired into endowed grammar schools, and an act of 1869 regulated these.

The educational outlook of the time could envisage only a dual system: simple essentials at day schools for the great majority of children; and more advanced education, largely by boarding schools, for the minority, especially for those who would proceed to the professions and services. For this latter provision Bedford, with the Harpur endowment, seemed to the government ideally suited. Bedford, it was thought, should cater for a school population drawn from far and wide (in those years of empire). Resentful Bedfordians objected to making 'an upper class boarding school for all England', while that staunch old liberal, the draper George Hurst, described it as 'plundering that which was intended for the necessities of the poor and giving it to the more wealthy'.

Bedford – and the Harpur Trust – were on the horns of a dilemma. Strait-jacketed by the government (by a scheme imposed in 1873), the Trust was limited for what was then called elementary education to two-elevenths of their income. The government had even tried to insist on a ceiling of £2,000 for expenditure in this category, saying – in the style of Canute – that Bedford's population 'can hardly increase very much more'. When, in spite of the government, Bedford did increase, the only way for elementary education to expand in Bedford was by setting up a school board. But Bedford, accustomed to leave all educational matters to the Harpur Trust, refused to face up to the situation. The Trust did manage to provide, in addition to the schools in the Harpur complex, additional elementary schools in Ampthill Road and Clapham Road. But by 1895 the Trust had 3,868 children in buildings designed for 3,500. At last in 1899 they had to refuse to admit any more children.

Some faint efforts were made by Bedford churches, but these were shortlived and unsatisfactory. When a Church Schools Association was promoted in 1896 by the mayor, it managed to collect only £149. In the end, a school board was set up in 1897. This built Goldington Road school and also one for Queens Park. Its responsibility was brief, however, for in 1902 a new education act gave educational responsibility to town councils. So the town council took over existing elementary schools, and later built Elstow Road school and the Silver Jubilee school.

Meanwhile, the 1873 Harpur Trust scheme had a marked effect on other education. From it, Bedford developed a special educational slant which it was to retain for seventy years, and which made it known throughout the world as an educational centre. The Harpur endowment income was now again rising, since Holborn was developing commercially. The former welfare expenditure had almost entirely ceased under the 1873 scheme: hall money (alms in mid-winter) had already been phased out; apprenticeship and marriage portions were an anachronism; only the almshouses were to continue, and were entitled to one-eleventh of Trust income. Thus the greater part of the available funds could be devoted to four schools: the two existing boys' schools (Grammar and Modern), with two companion girls' schools.

All four schools took boarders. Boarding had begun at Bedford as an encouragement to an active and able master to add to his income, and thus to improve his school, which improvement would benefit Bedford boys. But now boarding was considered – in the fashionable view of the day – an end in itself, and in the peak period of empire now approaching, Bedford schools, with their low fees were of great benefit to the many families whose fathers were serving overseas in the forces or in administration. A national paper (the *Daily News*) would even say in 1883 that Bedford was rapidly becoming the metropolis of education in England.

The boys' schools grew. At the Grammar School, already in 1858 some expansion westward on the existing site (the present Civic Theatre) had taken place; and again eastward in 1876 on the site of what had once been Woodward's brewery: and also in 1884 in new buildings nearby. But a new site was needed. By 1891 nearly twenty acres north of St Peter's had been secured, and there a large modern building was opened in that year – the field being already in use. The Modern School expanded on the Harpur Street site.

Meanwhile for girls a new building in Bromham Road (decorated for the occasion with evergreen arches) was opened in 1882 to accommodate both the girls' schools, each having about forty girls. Numbers increased so much that in 1892 the High School took over the whole building, while the Girls' Modern School moved into one of the buildings in St Paul's Square (the so-called Cowper building) vacated by the Grammar School. The core of the old Grammar School – Harpur's original building as refronted in the 18th century – was taken over by the corporation, and became the Town Hall.

Not only as boarders did children of overseas fathers come to Bedford. Many families came to live here. Bedford grew as a residential centre, and one with a special slant. Later an old boy remembered how every morning High Street saw a procession of he called the *haut ton*, all well turned out, but wretchedly poor, for families were large and pensions small. 'In one form of which I was a member, 17 had been born in India'. A brochure on Bedford in 1913 encourages incoming residents thus: 'society is just what Anglo-Indians have been accustomed to'. At the Town and County Club (1885) such new residents found a social centre.

Like attracts like: more educational establishments arrived in Bedford. A girls' boarding school called Howard College was run by Mrs Compton Burnett (reflections of it are found later in the caustic works of her daughter Ivy). Two new developments were a Froebel College in the Crescent by 1884, and (a great innovation for its day) the Physical Training College for girls run by Miss Stansfeld.

Considering the many boys, and later also girls, educated in Bedford who went overseas, it is not surprising that, by the end of the century, there were ten Bedfords overseas, mainly in the United States.

OTHER DEVELOPMENTS

More amenities followed, but not in every sphere. The most surprising gap in an educational town is the lack of public library provision (though Luton had a free library established in 1883 and soon taken over by the town council). The subscription library continued in what had been the Assembly Rooms (acquired in 1885 by that body with a cumbersome name, the Bedford Literary and Scientific Institute and General Library), and never was financially secure enough to provide a vigorous and expanding service. In the same building was a small amateur collection of antiquities. A larger collection grew at the Modern School from a nucleus given in 1884 by an old boy, Charles Prichard.

A historically minded mayor, F. A. Blaydes, from 1886 to 1893 studied and published some of the corporation's historical manuscripts, and issued a periodical publication, *Bedfordshire Notes & Queries*, which laid the foundation for later work. A Natural History Society was formed in 1875.

There were building developments. Prebend Street bridge was opened in 1883. In 1899 came a theatre, opened by Violet Vanbrugh. Other new buildings were the drill hall in Ashburnham Road, and a new Shire Hall to replace the inconvenient old Sessions House (it had been delayed so long that it was built just before the setting up of the County Council, which was soon to need more accommodation). St Paul's church had a new north aisle in 1884, opened by the Bishop of Ely, and in 1879 a carillon installed by public subscription (the transfer to the diocese of St Albans was made in 1914). Other church expansion went ahead in outlying areas: St Martin's in Clapham Road, Christ Church in Goldington Road, St Leonard's in Victoria Road, soon followed by All Saints in Iddesleigh Road and St Andrew's in Kimbolton Road; while the Salvation Army set up premises, and the Roman Catholic church was built in Brereton Road. The two political parties (conservative and liberal) built clubs (from 1885 Bedford had one MP only).

Civic consciousness showed in other ways. It was a period when towns began to put up visible tributes to their great men of the past. Bunyan's statue on St Peter's Green was presented by the Duke of Bedford in 1874. Twenty years later came that of Howard put up by public subscription. A beginning was made in setting up parks and gardens: the main park was opened in 1888, and a bandstand set up in 1903. Now that the river was no longer a commercial highway, the embankment's present transformation to an amenity area began. The suspension bridge was built in 1888. Active in all these improvements was Joshua Hawkins, five times mayor between 1883 and 1899.

Sport grew. There were two football clubs: the Rovers, 1876, and the Swifts, 1882; these amalgamated in 1886 to form the Bedford Rugby Football Club. Later (1897) came the Bedford Town Association Football Club. Bedford Rowing Club was formed in 1886, and the regatta was now well established and popular.

Art had its followers. Henry Stannard, a watercolour artist, came to Bedford and established an Academy of Arts in Prebend Street.[3] Many pleasant landscapes by him and his son, Henry Sylvester Stannard (who continued the Academy but in Dame Alice Street) are still extant. The Bedford Amateur Musical Society continued to flourish.

There was also more thought for the sick: a Nursing Association from 1896 raised money to pay for visiting nurses.

JUBILEE AND CORONATION

When the time came for Queen Victoria's Diamond Jubilee, thanksgiving services were held on Sunday 21 June 1897 under drizzle and clouds. But on Monday for the main celebrations there were balmy breezes and hot sunshine. Decorations were everywhere, and the *Bedfordshire Times* in its following issue included details for every shop in High Street and the main streets. The roasting of an ox on Cardington meadow, supervised by Bedford butchers, began at 5 am; it was said to be prime beef, perfectly cooked; old people brought an amazing diversity of crockery to collect their portions. After sports, 4,915 children sat down to tea. At night the river fête was 'pre-eminently brilliant'. Twenty thousand lamps were employed in the area, and the suspension bridge was made to look like the Rialto. The procession of boats took place at 9.30 pm, with two police boats in attendance, but 'excellent order was kept', and their intervention was not required. It was a day Bedfordians remembered for a long time.

When in June 1911 the occasion came for celebrating the coronation of George V, there was some muttering in the town that a public meeting ought to be called to make proposals, but the mayor said the town was too big for such a meeting to act effectively. Again the river was illuminated; there was tea for children in the park; and a Friendly Societies dinner in the Corn Exchange. And – since illustrations now were beginning to appear in newspapers, the *Bedfordshire Times* of 30 June gave a whole page of pictures of Bedford's celebrations.

11 NOTES
1. C.R.O., TLD 1.
2. See my *Harpur Trust*.
3. Information on the Stannards kindly given by Miss P. Bell.

12 Postscript

In this period Bedford nearly doubled, (1911: 39,183; 1971: 73,229), but since it was over sixty years the rate of increase was slower than in the previous hundred years. This time the town spread partly in high-rise flats, but mainly in vast suburban housing estates. A purpose-built Town Hall and County Hall arose. The town's boundaries were progressively widened: 1934, Goldington; 1967, parts of Clapham, Ravensden, Renhold, Cardington and Eastcotts. Then the local government reorganisation of 1974 revived a partial Victorian trend, and associated the town with most of rural north Bedfordshire in the North Bedfordshire Borough Council. Two world wars, economic development, and the end of empire brought many changes to Bedford. Some of these were common to all towns, especially county towns in the south-east; but some were either special to Bedford, or more pronounced in Bedford than elsewhere.

GENERAL CHANGES

Common to Bedford as elsewhere was the traffic revolution, which closed the railways to Cambridge and Hitchin, and greatly increased road traffic, so that Wing's bridge had to be doubled in width, and a new bridge built east of the town. Ever more complicated one-way street systems attempt to keep the torrent of cars moving, while multi-storey car parks are not able to keep them all off the streets. Fleets of comfortable buses bring villagers; at first these buses operated from a tiny site at St Peter's, but now from an extensive one nearer to the railway station. River communication from Bedford to the sea, now for recreation rather than commerce, is practicable again in 1978 with the restoration by the Anglian Water Authority of the last lock. Telephones, in their infancy in the last period (1896), are now almost universal, and the Bedford exchange controls over 100,000 lines.

With other towns Bedford has shared the de-personalising of industry, commerce and trade. Barnard's bank was taken over by the Westminster. The agricultural depression between the wars was too much for the Britannia Works (closed 1932). After the Second World War, more firms were established, including Texas Instruments from the United States. Multiple stores and supermarkets have ousted or taken over many old personal firms. There has been a similar trend in the entertainment industry; the theatre suffered from the introduction of five cinemas and then collapsed; while most of these cinemas eventually gave way to television.

Yet in some fields standardisation, here coupled with national or local control, has given vastly improved service. As has happened elsewhere to public utilities, Bedford Gas Company and Bedford Borough Electric Undertaking have given place to public corporations. Other services formerly provided by individual effort now come under national supervision. The health act of 1946 took over nursing, and now the hospital (greatly extended and modernised) functions in two wings, north and south (the former incorporating the old House of Industry). The volunteer fire brigade gave way to a public service in 1947.

In the field of libraries and museums, Bedfordians are today far better served. At last in 1935 Bedford implemented the public libraries act, and took over the former Assembly Rooms (the General Library expired quietly in 1958). This was just in time to receive in 1938 from the late Mott Harrison the bequest of his collection of Bunyan editions. In 1972 splendid new library premises were opened on the adjoining site (and the Assembly Rooms were renovated and restored to their original use under the name of the Harpur Suite).

Museum development came later. The Prichard Museum at the Modern School was carried on by masters (P. G. Langdon and then F. W. Kuhlicke); and when the latter retired from teaching, and the corporation at last in 1962 opened a museum on the Embankment in a former garage, Mr Kuhlicke continued for some years as director. Meanwhile the corporation had been encouraged by other private action to take responsibility in the field of art. Cecil Higgins (of the former brewing family) left his art collection to Bedford with a suggestion that it be placed in the former family home in Castle Close, and here a gallery of china, art and fine furniture was opened in 1949 and reorganised in 1977.

Less happy have been the effects of modernisation on what was left of the old town. A glance at *Bygone Bedford* reveals almost a different world existing within the period covered by the camera. Here are a few of our losses. The remains of the Franciscan friary went at the turn of the century. Nearly all of what was left of the old *George* inn has disappeared within the last thirty years. The *White Horse* inn gave place to Marks & Spencer. Sell & Willshaw went in 1964. The siting of churches in the centre of the town began to show its inconvenience when population had moved away, and St Paul Methodist church was a casualty when a new church on Newnham Avenue replaced it. Yet there has begun to be a revulsion in favour of keeping some of Bedford's past and Bedford's character, and the Bedford Society exists to promote this view. On the credit side are the restoration of St John's Hospital, where much of the mediaeval refectory was found intact, and the preserving of Blore's 1833 façade of the Harpur complex when the space behind it became a shopping centre; while the Harpur almshouses in Dame Alice Street have been modernised behind their existing façade (albeit this façade is *c.* 1890 and not original). What is now called College House (for Mander College) preserves for other uses the former dignified house of a Bedford burgess. Even some of the pleasanter houses of the last century in Bromham Road have been sympathetically restored and converted for office use.

One problem for the churches has been providing new buildings for worship in the large new development areas, while faced with difficulties in either maintaining historic buildings in the centre, or finding new uses for them. An instance of the latter is St Mary's, which it is hoped will become a historic centre. Another trend is that in Bedford, as elsewhere, many people see less relevance in denominational divisions; and since the last war Bedford Council of Churches has tried various activities, such as Good Friday processions, and exhibitions at the Public Library, and also organises Christian Aid Week. For Anglican purposes Bedford now has its own suffragan bishop.

Some changes have been, if not peculiar to Bedford, more pronounced than in many comparable towns.

One in which townsfolk may take justifiable pride is in the corporation's treatment of the river. Now, where formerly were coal and timber wharves and breweries, there are for a mile on either side tree-lined walks, sometimes bright with flowers. The process has taken most of this century, and was completed in 1977, Jubilee Year, with the disappearance of the Horne Lane brewery and the opening of Queen's Walk.

A more uncertain matter is the educational side of Bedford. Splendid new schools, such as the Pilgrim School, John Bunyan School, and Mark Rutherford School have arisen, and new premises have been provided for the College of Education (formerly Froebel) in 1950 and that of the College of Physical Education in 1952, while the Technical Evening Institute has turned into Mander College. But for the Harpur Trust a revolution in educational theory made difficulties. Compelled in 1873 to aim at producing a professional and administrative élite, the Trust found élitism now a smear word, and preference given to strict equality. It made efforts, especially by an agreement of 1971 with the County Council, to move towards a more general service without sacrificing its schools' best standards. Now all its four schools are independent; however, the financial advantage which accrues from the Harpur Centre (the development of the former Harpur complex in Harpur Street as a shopping centre) enables it still to offer help to local boys and girls of limited means.[1] Incidentally, the Girls' Modern School (now Dame Alice) moved out to new premises in Cardington Road in 1938, while more recently the Boys' Modern School moved to a splendid establishment in Manton Lane.

Lastly, Bedford is now a multi-racial town. The last census (1971) showed an immigrant population of 17.5 per cent. Out of 73,229 persons, nearly 12,000 were born outside the United Kingdom. Of these, rather more than half are of European descent (Italians, Poles and Irish); and the remainder came from the West Indies, India and Pakistan. In 1968 the Bedford International Friendship Association appointed an Asian liaison officer, and this work continues. Bedford was chosen in 1977 for a pilot education project under the European Economic Community for the teaching of Mother Tongue and Culture to immigrant children. In 1976 there was first held for United Nations Day in St Paul's church an all-faiths service, in which all races took part.

1. The Clerk has kindly supplied the following information. The Harpur Centre site of 3½ acres, bounded by Midland Road, Harpur Street and Horne Lane, was developed by the Trust as a shopping and office project. This increased the value of the asset from £1¾m to £9m by November, 1976. Three-quarters of the rent roll was sold to Merchant Bankers, Hambro, with the Trust retaining the freehold and 25 per cent of the rising rent roll in the future. The entire income from the Centre to the Trust is devoted to Harpur Scholarships for pupils with parents of limited means and to the almshouses. This replaces to some extent the school places formerly taken up by the Local Education Authority.

Mayors

?	John Slye	1380	Thomas Jourdon
?	John Brodeye	1381	Thomas Jourdon
?	Simon Barschot	1384	Thomas Jourdon
1288	John –	1385	Thomas Jourdon
1297	John Cullebere	1388	Thomas Jourdon
1301	John Wymond	1389	John Howden
1307	Nicholas le Feroun	1390	Thomas Jourdon
1312	John Mareschall	1392	William Broun
1313	John Atte Wall	1393	Thomas Jourdon
1314	John Cullebere	1398	Roger Tunstal
1315	Nicholas le Feroun	1400	Thomas Jourdon
1316	Nicholas le Feroun	1401	Thomas Jourdon
1319	John Atte Wall	1402	Thomas Jourdon
1322	Thomas Haliday	1404	William Coterstok
1324	Nicholas de Astwode	1406	Roger Tunstale
1325	Nicholas de Astwode	1407	Roger Tunstale
1327	Simon Cullebere	1408	William Goderstoke
1330	Simon Cullebere	1409	William Cothristoke
1331	Nicholas de Astwode	1411	John Tunstal
1334	Richard Frereman	1412	John Tunstal
1339	John le Marchal	1413	John Tunstal
1341	John le Marchal	1414	John Kent
1342	John le Marchal	1416	John Kent
1343	John le Marchal	1418	William Douve
1344	John Mareschal	1422	William Douve
1346	Walter de Perle	1423	William Douve
1347	Walter de Perle	1425	Thomas Kempston
1348	Henry Arnold	1426	Thomas Kempston
1349	John le Marchal	1428	Thomas Bull
1350	Henry Arnold	1429	John Frepurs
1352	John le Marchal	1432	Thomas Hunt
1354	Henry Arnold	1433	Thomas Hunt
1356	Henry Arnold	1435	Robert Wasselyn
1358	William de Kempston	1437	John Frepurs
1360	Henry Arnold	1438	William Hunte
1361	William de Kempston	1440	Thomas Kempston
1362	William de Kempston	1441	Robert Plomer
1363	William de Kempston	1443	William Bette
1365	William de Kempston	1444	John Frepurs
1367	John Bosom	1445	John Frepurs
1369	John Bosom	1446	Thomas Kempston
1372	Richard Frereman	1447	Thomas Kempston
1374	Richard Frereman	1448	Roger Yve
1379	Richard Frereman	1449	Roger Yve

1450	Thomas Bole	1537	John Baker
1453	John Arthur	1538	William Borne
1454	John Spery	1541	William Forde
1455	John Spery	1542	Peter Carre
1456	John Arthur	1543	Thomas Russell
1457	Thomas Kempston	1544	Henry Albony
	John Spery	1545	John Ward
1460	William Brytevyle	1546	John Williams alias Scott
1461	John Spery	1547	William Hall
1462	William Brytevyle	1548	Henry Fitzhugh
1406	William Comnoeur	1549	John Williams
1467	Walter Stotfold	1551	John Williams
1469	Robert Rotur	1554	William Halle
1470	William Chicheley	1555	John West, sr.
1471	Walter Stotfold	1556	Thomas Leighe
1472	Walter Stotfold	1558	William Bull
1475	William Chicheley	1559	Richard Lawrence
1476	Roger Sperling	1560	Humphrey Lawrence
1477	John Chapman	1562	Henry Lawrence
1478	John Gowlde	1563	Simon Beckett
1479	Philip Dyer	1564	Alexander Hunt
1480	William Paryse	1565	Robert Paradyne
1484	Thomas Hanchiche	1566	Henry Lawrence
1486	John Goold	1573	Henry Lawrence
1487	William Fitzhugh	1574	Alexander Hunt
1490	John Goold	1575	Thomas Hawes
1495	John Alwey	1576	Simon Beckett
1496	Thomas May	1577	John Mighton
1504	Simon West	1578	Robert Waller
1506	Robert Cokko	1580	Henry Lawrence
1507	William Payne	1581	Alexander Hunte
1508	Alexander Crowle	1583	John Mighton
1509	Robert Smyth	1584	Thomas Hawes, sr.
1510	Simon West	1585	Robert Waller
1511	Thomas Heche	1586	Thomas Abbys
1512	Thomas Knyght	1587	Thomas Hawes, jr.
1513	Richard Halam	1588	Alexander Hunte
1514	Simon West	1589	Richard Bell
1519	John Pateman	1590	Thomas Abbys
1520	Thomas Vinter	1591	Thomas Hawes, sr.
1521	Richard Halam	1592	Samuel Christye
1522	John Albony	1593	William Wilson
1527	Thomas Rowthe	1594	Robert Waller
1528	John Baker	1595	William Negus
1529	Thomas West	1596	Thomas Hawes, jr.
1534	Giles Lawrance	1597	Thomas Abbys
1535	Thomas Smyth	1598	John Stanton

1599	Simon Beckett	1646	John Grew
1600	William Negus	1647	John Hancocke
1601	Thomas Hawes, jr.	1648	John Faldo
1602	Thomas Hawes, sr.	1649	Henry Fitzhugh
1603	Robert Lawrence	1650	John Eston
1604	Thomas Abbys	1651	Robert Bell
1605	Robert Hawes	1652	William Faldo, sr.
1606	Simon Beckett, sr.	1653	Thomas Spencer
1607	James Payley	1654	John Crawley
1608	Jasper Chrystie	1655	Simon Beckett, sr.
1609	Thomas Hawes, jr.	1656	John Eston
1610	Thomas Hawes sr.		John Grew
1611	Peter Bamford		Robert Fitzhugh
1612	William Abbys	1657	Richard Mightnall
1613	Thomas Paradine	1658	John Hancock
1614	Simon Beckett	1659	John Eston
1615	John Goodhall	1660	Robert Bell
1616	Jacob Lawrence	1661	Simon Becket
1617	William Waller	1662	William Riseley
1618	Thomas Hawes, jr.	1663	John Crawley
1619	William Abbys	1664	William Faldo, sr.
1620	Robert Hawes	1665	John Crawley
1621	Robert Bamforth		John White
1622	Peter Bamforth	1666	William Faldo, sr.
1623	Thomas Spencer	1667	Francis Becket
1624	William Faldoe	1668	Thomas Underwood
1625	William Waller	1669	William Faldo, jr.
1626	William Abbys	1670	William Lane
1627	Steven Luxford	1671	Richard Mightnall
1628	John Spencer	1672	Thomas Paley
1629	Robert Bamforth	1673	John Crawley
1630	Thomas Waller	1674	John White
1631	William Waller	1675	William Becket
1632	Thomas Paradine	1676	Ralph Smith
1633	Thomas Hawes	1677	Simon Beckett, sr.
1634	William Abbys	1678	William Fenn
1635	Francis Bannester	1679	Robert Fitzhugh
1636	John Whitaker		William Bamforth
1637	John Spencer	1680	Anthony Bolton
1638	Robert Hawes	1681	Paul Bamforth
1639	John Eston	1682	John Paradine
1640	Thomas Hawes	1683	Paul Cobb, sr.
1641	Robert Bamforth	1684	Paul Cobb, sr.
1642	Robert Bell	1685	William Faldo, sr.
1643	William Paley	1686	Francis Becket
1644	Simon Beckett, sr.	1687	Thomas Underwood
1645	Francis Bannester		

1688	William Isaack	1731	Thomas Cave
	Paul Cobb	1732	Thomas Hawes
	Thomas Underwood	1733	Peter Haslewood
1689	William Becket	1734	Francis Walker
1690	John Eston	1735	Robert Battison
1691	Thomas Battison	1736	Thomas Edwards
1692	Ralph Smith	1737	Thomas Maddey
1693	John Paulin	1738	Gidney Phillips
1694	John Peck	1739	John Grey
1695	Richard Chichely	1740	Samuel Richardson
1696	George Maddy	1741	Robert Battison
1697	William Faldo	1742	Isaac Hayes
1698	John Deare	1743	John Hornbuckle
1699	John Kidd	1744	John Russell
1700	Thomas Wilkes	1745	John Webb
1701	Thomas Battison	1746	John Hill
1702	George Wagstaffe	1747	William Webb
1703	Henry White	1748	Samuel Richardson
1704	John Peck	1749	James Bailey
1705	John Fenn	1750	Gidney Phillips
1706	Thomas Underwood	1751	James Chamberlain
	Francis Walker	1752	Thomas Cave
1707	Thomas Day	1753	William Palmer
1708	Philip Negus	1754	Robert Richards
1709	Robert Crawley	1755	Gidney Phillips
1710	Thomas Underwood		Richard Cave
1711	William Faldo	1756	William Parker, sr.
1712	Richard Willis	1757	John Howard
1713	George Maddey	1758	Richard Cave
1714	John Kidd	1759	John Hill
1715	Thomas Battison	1760	Samuel Richardson
	Alexander Read	1761	William Webb
1716	David Ovray	1762	William Parker, jr.
1717	George Hawkins	1763	John Cave
1718	William Staines	1764	James Chamberlain
1719	Francis Okeley	1765	Thomas Knight
1720	Thomas Wilkes	1766	John Howard
1721	John Pulley	1767	Gidney Phillips
1722	Thomas Battison, jr.	1768	John Heaven
1723	Henry Fleming	1769	John Cawne
1724	Thomas Day	1770	Richard Cave
1725	William Bromsall	1771	William Parker, sr.
1726	William Lake, sr.	1772	Edward Chapman
1727	John Bardolph	1773	Gidney Phillips
1728	David Ovray	1774	John Cawne
1729	George Hawkins	1775	Gidney Phillips
1730	William Staines		John Parker

1776	Anthony Barton	1823	Francis Green
1777	Gidney Phillips	1824	Thomas Kidman
1778	John Palmer	1825	James Webb
1779	William Parker, jr.	1826	Charles Short
1780	Anthony Barton	1827	Charles Bailey
1781	Thomas Howard	1828	George Livius
1782	William Pateman	1829	William Long
1783	John Pheasant	1830	T. G. Elger
1784	John Cave	1831	Charles Bailey
1785	William Palmer	1832	G. P. Nash
1786	Thomas Partridge	1833	Thomas Wooldridge
1787	William Smith	1834	George Witt
1788	William Parker	1835	T. G. Elger
1789	William Smith	1836	Charles Short
1790	Thomas Clayton	1837	Charles Short
1791	Thomas Small	1838	T. G. Elger
1792	William Parker	1839	T. A. Green
1793	John Wing	1840	Robert Newland
1794	Thomas Cockman	1841	W. R. Mesham
1795	Peregrine Nash	1842	Joseph Browne
1796	John Day	1843	T. J. Green
1797	John Cooke	1844	T. J. Green
1798	Charles Webb	1845	Robert Newland
1799	Edward Chapman, jr.	1846	Alexander Sharman
1800	John Day	1847	Henry Leech
1801	William Smith	1848	Charles Higgins
1802	Isaac Elger	1849	C. F. Palgrave
1803	William Long	1850	C. F. Palgrave
1804	Francis Green	1851	William Williams
1805	William Campion	1852	William Williams
1806	Thomas Kidman	1853	William Blower
1807	Peregrine Nash	1854	Thomas Barnard
1808	John Wing	1855	George Hurst
1809	John Cooke	1856	W. W. Kilpin
1810	G. D. Yeats	1857	G. H. Miller
1811	Charles Short	1858	John Howard
1812	John Day	1859	John Howard
1813	William Long	1860	John Howard
1814	Francis Green	1861	John Howard
1815	Thomas Kidman	1862	Robert Couchman
1816	Charles Webb	1863	James Howard
1817	John Wing	1864	James Howard
1818	John Cooke	1865	W. J. Nash
1819	John Green	1866	W. J. Nash
1820	John Day	1867	T. T. Gray
1821	Charles Short	1868	T. T. Gray
1822	William Long	1869	A. E. Burch

1870	J. R. Bull	1915	F. R. Hockliffe
1871	James Coombs	1916	F. R. Hockliffe
1872	F. T. Young	1917	Harry Browning
1873	George Hurst	1918	F. R. Hockliffe
1874	George Hurst	1919	W. E. Sowter
1875	J. T. Hobson	1920	W. E. Sowter
1876	J. T. Hobson	1921	William Nicholls
1877	J. U. Taylor	1922	G. H. Barford
1878	George Hurst	1923	G. H. Barford
	T. G. E. Elger	1924	G. H. Barford
1879	J. E. Cutcliffe	1925	G. H. Barford
1880	J. T. Hobson	1926	G. H. Barford
1881	J. W. Hill	1927	William Nicholls
1882	Luke Cherry	1928	G. H. Barford
1883	Joshua Hawkins	1929	S. B. Morling
1884	Joshua Hawkins	1930	S. B. Morling
1885	Edwin Ransom	1931	G. H. Wells
1886	George Hurst	1932	S. B. Morling
1887	Joshua Hawkins	1933	H. R. Neate
1888	Joshua Hawkins	1934	H. R. Neate
1889	James Coombs	1935	H. R. Neate
1890	Joshua Hawkins	1936	W. E. Sowter
1891	James Coombs	1937	W. E. Sowter
1892	F. A. Blaydes	1938	Archibald Braggins
1893	George Wells	1939	Archibald Braggins
1894	George Wells	1940	A. M. Dudeney
1895	F. A. Blaydes	1941	A. M. Dudeney
1896	George Wells	1942	F. A. Rickard
1897	George Wells	1943	F. A. Rickard
1898	George Wells	1944	J. A. Canvin
1899	Hedley Baxter	1945	J. A. Canvin
1900	Henry Burridge	1946	J. A. Canvin
1901	Geoffrey Howard	1947	A. L. Nicholls
1902	Hedley Baxter	1948	A. L. Nicholls
1903	George Royle	1949	A. L. Nicholls
	E. L. Moulton	1950	Richard Turner
1904	Henry Burridge	1951	Richard Turner
1905	George Haynes	1952	C. Wickings-Smith
1906	George Haynes	1953	C. A. E. C. Howard
1907	S. L. Kilpin	1954	C. A. E. C. Howard
1908	E. L. Moulton	1955	R. G. Gale
1909	H. W. Longhurst	1956	R. G. Gale
1910	J. B. Hope	1957	A. A. Jones
1911	William Roff	1958	A. A. Jones
1912	Harry Browning	1959	C. N. Barrott
1913	Harry Browning	1960	A. H. Randall
1914	Harry Browning	1961	A. H. Randall

1962	A. G. Dawes	1971	Winifred M. Fowler
1963	G. R. Bailey	1972	Henry Rischmiller
1964	G. R. Bailey	1973	G. M. Bates
1965	R. A. Whittingham	1974	B. F. Dillingham
1966	T. B. Wooliscroft	1975	G. C. W. Beazley
1967	Ronald Sharman	1976	T. R. Donnelly
1968	K. J. R. Birtwistle	1977	Nora M. Polhill
1969	W. J. Martin	1978	Paul Hooley
1970	R. A. Whittingham		

Note:

When a mayor died or retired during his term of office, he was usually succeeded by the senior alderman.

Under the Local Government Act of 1972, followed by the setting-up of North Bedfordshire Borough Council, for the first year the mayor was mayor of Bedford town only, but since then the mayor has also been the chairman of the council.

The list of Mayors was compiled by Mr G. D. Gilmore, and is printed by permission of North Bedfordshire Borough Council.

Index

Holy Trinity, 126
Hook, Jn., 105
Hooley, Paul, 151
Hope, J. B., 150
Hornbuckle, Jn., 148
Hospitals, medical, 110–1; see also St. Leonard
Hospitals, religious, see St. John, St. Leonard
House of correction, 55, 98
House of Industry, 110, 121, 141
Household goods, 37, 39, 60, 68
Howard, C. A. E. C., 150; Geof., 150; Jas., 117, 123, 129, 149; Jn., 148; Jn. (industrialist), 115, 118, 121, 123, 127, 149; Jn. (philanthropist), 95, 137; Tho., 149
Howard College, 136
Howard Congregational church, see New Meeting
Howden, Jn., 145
Hudson, Ben., 66–7
Hull, Mary, 98
Hunt, Alex., 146; Fra., 98; Phil., 106, 112; Tho., 145; Wm. 145
Huntingdon, 13; Huntingdonshire, 89–90
Hurst, Geo., 121, 126, 129, 134, 149–50

Igranic Electric Co., 133
Immigration, 143
Improvement Commissioners, 109
Independents, 71–2, 75–6, 94–5; see also New Meeting, Old Meeting
Infirmary, see hospital
Inns, 99; Bear and Dog, 88; Bell, 39; Black Horse, 104; Castle, 88, 104; Chequers, 97; Christopher, 39; Cock, 39; Cresset, 39; Crown, 39; Falcon, 39; Fountain, 132; George, 39, 52, 133, 142; Hart, 39; Haycock, 104; Hearse and Horses, 104; Hop Pole, 112; Nag's Head, 104; New, 104; New Ship, 104; Peacock, 69, 88; Red Lion, 103–4; Rose, 88; Saracen's Head, 92, 104; Ship, 104; Shoulder of Mutton, 104; Sow and Pigs, 104; Swan, 39, 75, 83, 88, 99, 102–3, 117; Wheatsheaf, 99; White Horse, 133, 142; Wrestlers, 104
Isaac, 22
Isaack, Wm., 80, 82, 148

Jackins, Edw., 92
Jackson, Chas., 89; Geo., 105
Jarvis, T., 119
Jeffes, Agnes, 59
Jemmatt family, 79

Jennings, Fra., 90
Jews, 22, 38, 113, 127
John, King, 23–4
Johnson, Patience and Shadrach, 99
Jones, A. A., 150; Ralph, 61; Wm., 109
Jourdon, Tho., 145
Joye, Geo., 49; Tho., 39; Wm., 34–5

Kempston, 11; Geof., 40; Jn., 49; Tho., 145–6; Wm., 145.
Kent, Jn., 145
Kettering, 103
Kidd, Jn., 148
Kidman, Tho., 149
Kilpin, S. L., 150; W. W., 149
King's Ditch, 13, 18
Knight, Tho., 49, 146, 148
Kuhlicke, F. W., 141

Lace, 57, 82, 86, 120–1
Lake, Wm., 148
Lane, Sam., 82; Wm., 147
Langdon, P. G., 141
Langhorne, Wm., 69
Lansdowne Road, 132
Lawrance, Lawrence, Giles, Hen. and Humph., 146; Jacob, 147; Ric. and Robt., 147
Leech, Hen., 149
Leicester, 26, 67
Leigh, Tho., 146
Leith, Alex., 94, 99
Lester, Chas. and Tho., 122
Library, 98, 128, 136–7, 141
Lime kiln, 37
Lime Street, 37
Lincoln, 26
Littledale, Hen., 116
Livius, Geo., 149
Long, Wm., 101, 104, 109, 119, 149
Longhurst, H. W., 150
Lucy, Edm., 48
Luke, Nich., 48, 55; Ol., 48; Sam., 66–7; Walt., 48
Luton, 19, 24, 42, 50, 66, 112
Luxford, Ste., 64, 147

Mabbott, Ric., 70
Mace, 56
Maddy, Geo., 148; Tho., 148
Maldon, Jn., 40
Manchester, 121
Mantel, Jn., 126
Market, 14, 21, 55, 58, 86
Marshall, Jn., 145
Martin, W. J., 151
Matilda, 19, 23, 30
Matthew, Jas., 86; Tim., 127